What people are saying about

Reeves and Schuster

Stephen Collins is an incredibly gifted teacher and Sam Collins is a talented storyteller. Their book, *Reeves and Schuster: Lessons for Leaders in a Sitcom World*, offers a fun read filled with practical wisdom for being an effective servant leader. Well worth the time invested!
George Green IV, CEO and President, Water Mission

Stephen and Sam Collins have teamed up and written an entertaining leadership book, *Reeves and Schuster: Lessons for Leaders in a Sitcom World*. This is a unique approach to share the principles of leadership, told in a storybook format. They note in the book, "The people you lead, follow, and collaborate with will most likely be your source of greatest joy and frustration." As a leader, you help determine the trajectory of the joy or frustration. Stephen has helped MAP International train our leaders through the Servant-Leadership model to achieve our organizational goals.
Steve Stirling, CEO and President, MAP International and author of *The Crutch of Success*

Reeves and Schuster integrates information and humor to provide insights on a proven leadership concept. The story had me laughing out loud and we in business all know we need more humor in our reading and business practices. Good work!
Gene K. Ontjes, Chick-fil-A franchise owner/operator for 49 years

Reeves and Schuster

Lessons for Leaders in a Sitcom World

Reeves and Schuster

Lessons for Leaders in a Sitcom World

Sam Collins and Stephen Collins

BUSINESS
BOOKS

Winchester, UK
Washington, USA

JOHN HUNT PUBLISHING

First published by Business Books, 2024
Business Books is an imprint of John Hunt Publishing Ltd., No. 3 East St., Alresford,
Hampshire SO24 9EE, UK
office@jhpbooks.com
www.johnhuntpublishing.com
www.johnhuntpublishing.com/business-books

For distributor details and how to order please visit the 'Ordering' section on our website.

Text copyright: Sam Collins and Stephen Collins 2022

ISBN: 978 1 80341 442 3
978 1 80341 443 0 (ebook)
Library of Congress Control Number: 2022923037

A CIP catalogue record for this book is available from the British Library.

Design: Lapiz Digital Services

UK: Printed and bound by CPI Group (UK) Ltd, Croydon, CR0 4YY
Printed in North America by CPI GPS partners

We operate a distinctive and ethical publishing philosophy in
all areas of our business, from our global network of authors to
production and worldwide distribution.

Contents

To Anita, who makes everyone in the family a better leader
and a better person

Acknowledgments

For both of us, this book is the result of so many people who invested in our education and experiences. We have been truly blessed to know leaders and teachers who gave us opportunities to experiment, fail, and grow.

Thank you to our team of early readers who provided the needed direction and encouragement for us to experiment with this format.

We want to express our appreciation to all the folks who have invested their passion, talents, and time to create the opportunities Lead International and its affiliates have had to share leadership principles to audiences around the world. Your faith in the endeavor allowed us to continue to do something we love.

We also want to acknowledge all the workshop participants who shared their best ideas, questions, and experiences. You always made it fun and kept us growing. Those conversations sharpened our understanding and made us hopeful of a better future.

A special thank you to the organizations whose mission called them to serve those most in need. It has been a blessing and an inspiration to support your teams and learn from your commitment to making a better world.

Thanks to our parents and grandparents who faithfully supported our calling to live and travel far from home and encouraged us to share what we learned.

We also greatly appreciate Claire for contributing her insights to the project. More importantly, her adventures as a video journalist, daughter, and sister have made us better at teaching and storytelling.

Thank you, Anita, whose love always protects, always trusts, always hopes, and always perseveres. She models what matters most as a wife and mom.

Finally, thanks to the team at John Hunt Publishing for their needed expertise and encouragement.

Introduction

I still remember my first encounter with real organizational leadership nearly 4 decades ago. Following my graduation from university, I enthusiastically accepted a management job working with a large manufacturing company. My business education had not appeared overly academic to me, and I felt ready to tackle the real-world problems found on the factory floor. However, since I had only lived in the academic world, I was completely unqualified to make that determination. The mastery I believed I had of classic motivation and leadership theories provided little assistance when confronted with thirty subordinates who had spent years developing their own theories of life, including how much physical, mental, and emotional energy they should invest in an 8-hour shift. There was nothing intentionally malicious in their approach. The workers had a role to play as did their supervisors in this drama on the factory floor.

Like a reluctant actor who has been pushed onto the stage, I spent the first few weeks trying to get a copy of the script as everyone else already seemed to be quite comfortable with their roles. I first turned to my fellow supervisors. Just about all of them had begun on the other side of the divide as "labor." Through hard work and a demonstrated aptitude for leadership, each of them, years earlier, had accepted an invitation to join the management team. Theirs was a different perspective compared with my academic (outsider) one.

When asked to share some practical leadership tips, each one reacted with the confidence of a Zen master before a recently arrived novice. Office doors were closed, coffee cups filled, and we each settled in for a lengthy discourse. While most of these individuals had not been afforded great educational opportunities, they still weaved leadership theories, academic disciplines, and compelling narratives with the skill of

Dostoyevsky. I sat wide-eyed as they presented the primary tenets of theology, psychology, and sociology through their stories touching on the broad spectrum of the human condition. Business classes were never this raw or gritty.

One impromptu group discussion deep into a late evening shift stands out. Several of the supervisors had, at length, identified what they believed to be the core leadership problem – the people they supervised. Everyone eagerly contributed examples from their experiences like poker players confidently raising their bets. I sat silently in the corner wondering how to get off this downbound train. And then Howard, all 6 foot 5 inches, stood up from his chair and slowly moved to the door. He was close to retirement age and I had never seen him do anything quickly. As he reached the door, he said, "You know what I think?" and then paused. I don't know if it was for dramatic effect or if he was just catching his breath, but the room grew still. "If it doesn't have something to do with people, it is just not worth doing." If the mic drop had been a thing in those days, that would have been Howard's moment. Instead, the room drew silent after his departure as everyone realized Howard had won the hand.

Answering questions like "What is really going on around here?" and "How do I contribute?" may consume a great deal of energy for those new to the workforce, but is still critical to anyone trying to lead. A big part of how you answer the questions will depend on whether you see people as the problem or the purpose. Even when you get the vision and strategy right, which is emphasized in business education, you will discover that success will be much more dependent on your understanding of human nature. The people you lead, follow, and collaborate with will most likely be your source of greatest joy and frustration.

Many insightful books have been written using stories or fables to highlight organizational challenges and identify useful approaches for positively influencing those around us. Most of these books attempt to provide a realistic context that approximates our common experiences in work environments, allowing us to quickly identify with the situation and the cast of characters. The story that follows takes a slightly different approach.

We decided to utilize a format that has proven to be a great illuminator of the human condition, the sitcom. Sitcoms offer a unique form of storytelling. The most humorous characters are almost always flaw-driven and even those with pure motives are easily influenced by pride and fear. The most ordinary situations of life get blown out of proportion by coincidences of fate and a cascade of poor decision-making.

While the primary intent of the sitcom is to make us laugh, the best ones also make us think. Growing up in the 60s and 70s, I spent way too much time watching and re-watching sitcoms. If I had spent the same amount of time reading science books or learning foreign languages, there might be an Ivy League address on my resume. The TV watching of my childhood certainly shaped my understanding of working relationships and the adult world in general. Classic American series like *The Andy Griffith Show*, *The Mary Tyler Moore Show*, and *MASH* provided deep insights into the tensions and opportunities created in close-knit working teams (long before *The Office* and *Parks and Recreation*); insights I never realized until I entered the work world and saw that with a little bit of exaggeration and imagination, my colleagues could star in their own workplace comedies.

There is one particular comedy we would like to single out and this one pre-dates radio and TV shows. PG Wodehouse's "Jeeves Stories" first appeared in print in 1915 and followed the misadventures of Bertie Wooster, a likable member of the idle rich, and his quite capable valet, Jeeves. The successful British series of the 90s starring Hugh Laurie and Stephen Fry created a popular following of the characters and helped make Jeeves a name synonymous with a clever manservant. Most of their stories follow a similar plot line with Wooster getting ensnared in a problem requiring Jeeves to come to the rescue.

While Wodehouse proved an important influence, we wound up taking our characters in a very different direction, while following similar sitcom tropes. Situations start as plausible and quickly devolve into the unlikely. The outrageous behaviors by characters are clear to a few but never to the one demonstrating the behavior. Resolutions to problems often appear suddenly and without warning. Sometimes, characters grow from their experiences, but more likely revert to deep-seated attitudes and habits.

And, of course, most sitcoms center around one character who attempts to project rationality into the situation. While this character possesses their own unique strengths and weaknesses, they provide the best hope for resolving whatever problem has been created by or thrust upon the cast.

In our story that is Calvin Schuster, a professor of management at Saint Foy's College, an institution with a steady stream of leadership challenges. Schuster would prefer the quiet life of an academic but finds himself tasked with solving whatever problem befalls the school. He may start each assignment with a great deal of reluctance, but the opportunity to apply his theories eventually fuels his enthusiasm. Accompanied by his eager to please and a bit overly practical teaching assistant, Reeves, and surrounded by a cast of characters who don't always behave as the textbooks predict, the professor discovers the messiness of leadership, but more importantly, the purpose of leadership.

Each "episode" emphasizes one of five fundamental areas where leaders must learn and refine their skills throughout their careers: change, communication, negotiation, innovation, and decision-making. While these are complex topics and this book isn't here to provide a comprehensive dive into each of them, our stories capture some of the universal aspects of human nature, as well as proven approaches that can be tried. At the end of each story, we summarize foundational principles and best practices.

Finally, an important reason for choosing to communicate these leadership lessons in this format was the opportunity to work with my son, Sam. As a screenwriter, his works span a range of genres but always illustrate our common hopes and fears. As usually the first person to read his initial drafts, I always appreciate how his stories highlight our need for growth and a belief in a better future, which are at the heart of leadership. He also is much more in touch with the sitcoms of today. Sam took my notes on a few management principles and created the characters and storylines that illustrate what makes leadership challenging, humorous, and rewarding.

Since that initial introduction to organizational leadership at the manufacturing company, I have lived and traveled all over the world, learning and teaching about leadership and management. The two questions I ask to determine the success of any training engagement are, "Did we have fun?" and "Did we learn something new?" Hopefully, you will answer yes to both when you finish this book.

Reeves in the Dugout

Prologue:
I have to imagine I was a sore sight, in my bathrobe attempting to make an all but raw potato edible through copious amounts of salt, pepper, and paprika. It wasn't until the visitor came that I had to deal with someone actually witnessing the sight.

"Are you in, Cal? Your doorbell's broken again."

I, of course, immediately recognized the voice as that of Jesse McNamara, the assistant dean of Saint Foy's College, my current employer. I, of course, also recognized, based on the tenaciousness of the knocking, that my visitor was not here to give me good news.

"Come on in. The door's unlocked."

Jesse entered; her brittle frame soaked in rainwater. We exchanged impolite glances at each other's unfortunate states before I finally had the nerve to break the silence.

"Forgot your umbrella?"

She grabbed the towel from the kitchen counter and patted down her face as she replied, "Forgot my car."

"I might need some elaboration."

"I've been using a faculty vehicle for the past week or so while mine was in the shop. I received a call yesterday that my car was ready to be picked up, but with no one to drive me there, I was forced to stick with one of the beat-up ones the college owns."

"No one could drive you?" I asked incredulously.

"Everyone was busy and, unfortunately, my car is where I keep my umbrella."

"That doesn't explain why you couldn't catch a cab."

"With everyone getting colds this season, I wasn't about to take my chances with a complete stranger's car. Say what you will about the moral and intellectual fiber our college attracts, but at least we're all hygienic."

It was true Saint Foy's was not known for providing a particularly "Ivy League" experience. It was started around the turn of the century by the well-to-do Charles Boyle, who had inherited a great deal of wealth from his parents and had no idea what to spend it on. Seeing the dearth of education in Culpepper, Maine, he set out to provide affordable higher education to those less fortunate. He founded the institution on the motto *a maiore ad minus*, a Latin phrase meaning "from the greater to the smaller," a call for equality regardless of wealth. Unfortunately, Saint Foy's wound up embodying a different Latin phrase, *errare humanum est*, "to err is human." Or perhaps an American expression would be the best fit of all, "you get what you pay for."

The esteemed Mister Boyle had not accounted for the significance leadership plays in a college, believing that simply hiring talented professors would be all it took to provide students with the opportunity to advance in their lives. While the teachers had certainly brought with them a great deal of experience and knowledge, they failed to work together as one team on a united quest, to educate the student body on matters of business.

A proper dean can make all the difference; someone to keep people on the right track, using compatible teaching styles to optimize student learning. This well-meaning, but unfortunate mistake has led to a grand tradition of leadership blunders that persists to this day at Saint Foy's College. I could only imagine my visitor was here to inform me of the latest one.

"Someone your age and...stature...really shouldn't be out in the rainfall like this," I said.

"I wouldn't have to come over in person if you would answer your blasted phone."

"I'm conducting an experiment. I read an article the other day that said people can't concentrate more than a few minutes at a time because we have changed the way our brains work with the need to be constantly checking social media posts and emails. So, I decided to test myself to see how long I could concentrate without any interruptions."

"How'd the experiment go?"

"Haven't started it yet. I figured my results would be more objective if I started it undistracted and I still have half a season of *Ted Lasso* ahead of me, so..."

"So, you disconnected your phone and spent all day watching TV?"

"My Apple trial ends tomorrow. I was in a bit of a rush."

"You could always just pay for the shows you watch like the rest of us."

"Unfortunately, money is a bit tight right now. Everything's going toward rent for the foreseeable future."

"What about your flatmate? That Crenshaw fellow?"

"I'm afraid Marion's left me."

"What?"

"Found a better job offer from Rodhelm College."

"Rodhelm?" she puzzled. "They're in almost as dire straits as *we* are financially. I can't imagine they offered him too great a raise."

"It wasn't about the money; not entirely, although from what I understand they are paying him a bit more. No, the main reason was that Marion felt Rodhelm fit his need for a 'professional environment' better than could be found around here."

"Unfortunately, I don't think you've got much of an argument against that, especially with what I'm here to discuss."

Jesse took the seat opposite me, her dour disposition leading me to believe she might not even remember to ask why I was in such a sorry state.

"Our good Dean Northum has given me an unusual charge. I'm afraid you'll have to contribute to its completion as well. The board of trustees is coming for a visit and Northum has it in him to impress them in some fashion they wouldn't expect."

"So, what kind of surprise are they in for?"

"Baseball."

"He's going to have them play baseball?"

"No. They'll be the audience. It's *us* who are going to put on the baseball game."

"But...Jesse, Saint Foy's doesn't have a baseball team. We haven't had one for decades. Our entire athletic department comes down to nothing more than frisbee players."

"Yes, but what we have to offer doesn't provide much of a spectacle, does it? The dean has it in him to transform those frisbee players into a proper fighting force."

"And we're the ones tasked with this job?"

"I'm sorry to say. I rushed over here right after he told me, even with the rain...well, right after I had failed to convince him it was a terrible idea, that is."

I sat there flummoxed at the situation. Those disc-tossers were never going to stand a chance against any *real* team.

"Northum has already arranged a game against players from Rodhelm College."

Now them, on the other hand, we may have a chance against.

"So, now that you know the story behind my unfortunate appearance, what's *your* excuse?"

Drat! I was hoping she had been too focused on this new predicament to ask me.

"Well, it ties back to my flatmate situation."

"How's that?"

"After Marion left, I found myself with three possibilities: convince him this university was a prestigious institution worth staying at..."

"Clearly that wasn't going to work."

"... move into a cheaper studio apartment..."

"Given the length of your legs, I doubt you'd fit in one."

"... or, the third option, Reeves."

"Reeves? Your TA?"

"That Reeves. Turns out he needed a place to stay and offered to move in."

"Reeves and Professor Schuster living together? I wouldn't have expected to see that happen."

"Until Marion left, I would have thought it rather unlikely as well."

"There's a bit of a salary difference between the two of you, isn't there?"

"Well, he isn't paying quite fifty percent of the bills or rent. He pays enough that I can afford to stay here and offered to take on some responsibilities to offset the difference."

"What kind of responsibilities?"

"Cooking, cleaning, the general household chores I used to split with Marion."

"So, it's a bit like having a live-in butler?"

"Not quite. A TA like Reeves doesn't entirely fit the expectations of a butler."

"I'm sure he's eager to please."

"Oh, that isn't the problem. He's a fine chap; does his best, a hard worker...The problem is he's too much of a TA, even outside the classroom. The job of a TA is to take the instructions I provide and use them to grade tests and papers, things like that; occasionally do some research for me or retrieve a file... For someone with his literal mind, he is ideal for such tasks."

"What does this have to do with your raw meal?"

I sat back, rubbing my eyes in frustration.

"I was giving a lecture yesterday on preparation versus action. I used the example of Albert Einstein, who once said that if given an hour to solve a problem, he would spend the first fifty-five minutes analyzing the question. Turns out he was paying very close attention to my words, but perhaps not to their practical application."

"And the potato?"

"I asked him to cook it for me an hour ago. He spent most of that time researching how stoves work before sticking it in with five minutes to go."

"Oh dear."

"Now I'm stuck with a practically raw potato for supper."

"And what of your clothes?"

"Unfortunately, he took the same attitude toward doing the laundry."

to be continued...

Part 1:

Although a snug fit, the billiards table nestled closely by the coffee table in my unfortunately small living room. I was practicing my breaking when Reeves entered.

"Professor Schuster…"

"Yes, Reeves?"

"I finally finished moving my things in. I wanted to thank you again for the room."

"No need to thank me. It's a trade-off, after all."

"I still appreciate it."

His attention turned to the coffee table, covered in pictures of Saint Foy's frisbee team.

"I think I recognize a few of these."

"You should. They're all students. Some of them are in our classes."

"Oh, yes. Now I see," he said, picking up one of them. "Jonathan Frewer. I think you gave this one a failing grade on his last paper."

"I can't seem to remember that one."

"It was on the importance of recruiting selectively. I believe he argued that nitpicking through someone's resume was inefficient, citing your lecture on Ernest Shackleton who, when hiring the crew for his Antarctic expedition, interviewed the applicants based on his gut instincts, what kind of feel he got from them to determine if they were right for the job. Why did you fail him again, sir?"

"Because Shackleton's ship got stuck in the ice and they had to turn back."

"Oh, yes. That explains it."

Honestly, the use of Shackleton's voyage in a paper on recruiting selectively could have earned a much higher grade if Frewer had bothered analyzing the story more critically. My lecture was not on how a speedy recruitment process is more efficient than a highly deliberate one. It was on the importance of vision in the recruiting process, itself. Shackleton put out an ad looking for applicants interested in a job involving bitter cold and constant danger (and only added honor and recognition in case of success at the end.) This ensured that the only sailors to apply were the ones who shared his vision, thus allowing for a faster recruitment process. Frewer seemed to think the takeaway was the importance of going with your gut.

"So why *are* you putting these pictures all over the coffee table?"

"Because the school's trustees are coming for a visit, and Dean Northum has charged us with putting on a baseball game to impress them."

"But these are frisbee players."

"They're the closest thing we have to a baseball team. Besides, there must be some overlap between the two sports; running, throwing…If we select the right players for this team and give them proper coaching, I have every confidence we can transform them into a respectable unit by the end of the week."

"The end of the week?"

"That's when the game is scheduled."

Ideally, we would have a greater time period to get the team together. Our limited number of days was more than enough to recruit the players but would likely not be enough to properly get them in the right mindset. People respond best to change when the facilitators of that change, their leaders, can work with them and encourage communication; learning what their ideas are and personalizing the experience. We lacked the time for any of that.

"Who will they even be playing against?" Reeves asked.

"The opposing team will be coming from Rodhelm College."

"I wasn't aware Rodhelm had much of an athletic division."

"That's our one saving grace. I'm banking on us looking good by comparison."

"You know, Professor, I happen to have played a bit of baseball back in the day."

"Then you will be the perfect choice for assistant coach."

"Oh...Uh, yes, sir. If that's where you believe I'll be best suited."

I set the pool cue down to join Reeves at the coffee table to continue our conversation, "That's the trick then, isn't it? Finding the right people and putting them in the right places. I firmly believe that the best leaders always start with the 'who' question."

"Why is that?"

"Think back to my lecture on Shackleton."

"You told it with such enthusiasm, sir."

Part of my appreciation for Reeves as my TA came from his adoration of my lectures. He did not always fully understand them, but it was nice to know there was at least one person in the lecture hall who cared what I was saying.

"While the journey was ultimately a failure in that his crew never reached their destination, they only managed to survive the months of exposure to the Arctic wilderness thanks to his leadership. This leadership would not have been possible with a poorly hired crew. He selected people that he was able to get to trust him through thick and thin. When the voyage went wrong and the ice made it likely they would starve or freeze to death, he led them to safety."

"Isn't that more an observation on his survival skills than on his crew's trust in him?"

"A leader that is always right is easy to trust. That wasn't the case with Shackleton, though. No, he led them on multiple escape attempts that proved unsuccessful. A different crew might have written him off as a failed leader, but he picked the right people who would stick with him throughout his mistakes. People might want a leader who will never err, but that rarely happens, and I doubt I'll be an example of such an exception.

We need players who can power through their mistakes as well as mine."

"So, what sort of qualities should we look for in these players?"

"There are the surface-level qualities of course. Take Henry Muldoon here," I said, picking up Henry's photo, "muscular arms, tall frame. He'll be an ideal pitcher, I'm sure."

"Geoffrey Catspin has legs almost as long as yours."

"Means he'll be a fine runner. Maybe outfield."

"What about beyond the surface level, sir? What else are you looking for?"

"I'm sure you recall my lectures discussing Patrick Lencioni's book, *The Ideal Team Player*. In it, he highlighted three qualities: humility, hunger, and intelligence."

"I'm sure Henry will fit 'hunger' at least. Not sure about the other two."

"Unfortunately, I see a great deal of compromise necessary for this process. The ideal team member possesses all three qualities. With most of these boys, we can only probably find one, maybe two if we're lucky with a few. We'll have to grab roughly equal amounts of players who demonstrate one quality as the others, and then they'll be able to compensate for each other's weaknesses."

"Was that in Lencioni's book as well?"

"No, I'm just an optimist."

"I think Shackleton would probably be considered one as well."

"I'm not a superstitious man, but I'd prefer you not to jinx this."

"Yes, sir."

"Now, these three principles are not required in a general sense. For example, none of these players need to know calculus to fill the intelligence quota. The important thing is that they are people-smart. They need to get along well together, take direction, and work as one. A team victory must be viewed as a personal one and vice-versa. Humility, meanwhile, means that we need them to recognize their weaknesses as well as they do their strengths, while also keeping their egos in check."

"How will you go about that?"

"Are you familiar with Stanley Kubrick's *Full Metal Jacket*?"

"That's one of my favorite war films."

"Well, just do whatever the drill sergeant in the film did and I'm sure they'll fall in line."

"Is that wise, Professor? I feel like they'll accept your leadership better if they like you."

"I've already thought that one through quite thoroughly, Reeves. While you break down their wills until their egos are nothing more than puddles of mush, I'll be the beloved head coach there to guide them with words of encouragement and motivational speeches more or less lifted from James Earl Jones in *Field of Dreams*, or maybe even Kenneth Branagh from his performance as Shackleton. What was that line in the film? 'For sudden the worst turns the best to the brave.'"

"So, if your plan works out, they'll despise me and love you?"

"Glad you're keeping up, Reeves."

"What of the third quality you mentioned; hunger?"

"That doesn't refer to literal hunger so much as it refers to ambition. They must be driven to excel, to want a victory as much as either of us. Dean Northum is counting on them. I can guarantee they'll feel the proper hunger needed to spring into action and do whatever it takes to win."

"I get it. They won't just be playing for a victory. They'll be playing for the pride of the school, for Dean Northum, for you, for me, and for the spirit of the sport."

"No. They'll be driven because we'll mainly select frisbee players in need of extra credit."

"That sounds much more pragmatic, sir. I'll start working on a list."

Reeves left the room to grab pen and paper while I gave the pictures another look, wondering how in over my head I was. I had hardly even played baseball since high school almost twenty years ago. Perhaps this was doomed from the start. I felt I would require everything I had ever learned on leadership for this task if I was to make my academic experience somehow translate into good coaching.

"Are you ready now?"

Reeves' reentrance snapped me out of my existential dread and I was once again ready to talk baseball.

"Reeves, the name of the game is strategy; namely, the strategic fit. We need nine players to fill out a field, and each one fits a specific purpose. We don't need everyone to be good at everything. It's like Isaiah Berlin's parable of the fox and the hedgehog. The fox is crafty, fast, strong, and agile. The hedgehog has one edge in the animal kingdom; it can curl into a ball, and nothing can touch it. It doesn't matter what the fox attempts, once that hedgehog is in its ball, it is impossible for the fox to successfully attack it."

"So, how will that translate here?"

"Baseball is the perfect sport for individual skills. Some players must be good at catching, some at running, and some at batting. We need to identify everyone's unique hedgehog skill and fit them into the overall strategy. We already went over Henry Muldoon and Geoffrey Catspin. How about Martin Wozniak?"

"He's sort of a gangly fellow, isn't he?"

"But he has aim. If you've ever seen him toss a frisbee, you know he has great hand-eye coordination."

"I can't imagine he has much force though."

"He won't need much force if we put him on second base. Remember, we're looking for hedgehogs, not foxes. The important thing is that they all work together in a way that compensates for their weaknesses and leverages their strengths. Someone has force. Another has aim. Another has speed."

"Should we consider looking for players who already have some baseball experience?"

His suggestion caught me off-guard.

"Now that you mention it, that would probably be a smart move."

I began wondering, could it be I had underestimated Reeves? That, in spite of his lack of thorough understanding of management matters, he might actually have possessed great insight I had yet to tap into?

"With his hair spiked up, Henry kind of looks like a hedgehog, doesn't he?"

His last statement made me reconsider that theory.

to be continued...

Part 2:

Regardless of being left to gather dust for the better part of fifty years, Saint Foy's baseball field cleaned up respectably once the lines were chalked and the gopher holes filled in. The bases were set. The equipment was out. I was hoping that the appearance of care and organization would demonstrate a commitment to the cause. These changes, even the small ones, would give the players a real sense of being a baseball team. I had even looked into getting a hotdog vendor to show up and add that extra layer of atmosphere.

Now all that we needed was for the players to arrive. I had set the meeting time for 9:30 sharp.

....

By 10:15, the final team member had shown up and we could begin. I approached the bleachers where they sat, Reeves behind me, and cleared my throat.

"Better late than never, I guess. I hope everyone's in good spirits this morning."

"Hey, Professor, what are we doing out here?" I heard Terrance Lawson, my proposed third baseman, ask with an air of defiance.

"Today, I'm here to present you with an exciting opportunity; a chance at a new athletic venture to boost school morale. I'm talking about that great American pastime, baseball."

The lack of response was expected, yet still discouraging. I had to reassure myself that adapting to change is, by definition, a process, and one that begins with awareness of what the change means, which is where the players were at. In this stage of the process, the new situation brought about by the change had yet to sink in, meaning most of them were probably working out their escape routes as I spoke.

The next stage of the process is forming a mental image of what the change means, followed by hands-on experience dealing with it. I had to pick my words carefully to get them to move on to these stages.

"Each of you has been selected based on a number of factors; your speed, your strength, your athletic history, and, for some of you, your need for extra credit to pass the semester."

This last line managed to perk up their attention. Their faces clearly showed they had entered the "what's in it for me?" part of adapting. They had accepted a new change in their plans for the week. Unfortunately, this is often a still-pessimistic part of the process; one where the people entering their new situation see it as a problem; an obstacle to be overcome, rather than an opportunity for improvement. I had to reel them in. I needed some form of engagement. Fortunately, Henry Muldoon lobbed me an easy one.

"Why do you want us to play baseball?"

"Dean Northum has us scheduled to play a game against Rodhelm College this Saturday when the board of trustees will be visiting campus. He believes it will provide an example of Saint Foy's fighting spirit as well as a source of entertainment for our guests."

"So, this is really about making Dean Northum look good at our expense?" Henry once again inquired.

"Don't think of it as being for the dean. Think of it as being for yourselves, for your school, for me. This is not just about impressing someone. This is about victory, about the pride of accomplishment."

I could tell my words were doing little to motivate them.

"It's about showing up those stuck-up players at Rodhelm."

This proved to be my strongest selling point as cheers of agreement echoed from the team, whose players had lost their last frisbee match against Rodhelm. I quickly disregarded my other intended talking points to focus on our shared enemy.

"This is about showing them they aren't better than us. This is about proving our school doesn't play second-fiddle to their ilk."

The further cheers confirmed I had moved us into the visualization stage, where those involved start imagining their situation during the change. In this case, the players were visualizing the sorry faces of the opposing team. The next stage would be when we actually took steps to reach this victory, which led me to the next stretch of my speech.

"If we want to win, that means practice, practice, practice. I know this isn't how you would ideally be spending the next few days, but it's what's necessary to ensure Rodhelm's demise. I've brought over some equipment: gloves, caps, uniforms...They're currently in the locker room. I want you to head over and find what fits you. Try not to scuff up the stuff that doesn't. I'm still hoping to get the deposit back on all this when we're done."

The players got up and headed for the locker room. I hoped having them put on uniforms for the first time would be a quick and easy way to change their identities from frisbee players to a baseball team. Small changes like this have the potential to create shifts in how people view their situation.

I opted not to give them too much time getting ready, knowing they would be more likely at this stage to bond over their shared issues with their predicament. Nothing encourages comradery quite like when everyone's in agreement about how much they don't like their situation. I decided to send Reeves after them to see if that was the case.

"Let's get going!" I shouted. "When you're done in there, meet back here in ten minutes on the mark."

....

Thirty minutes later, the last of them had returned and I had them playing catch with each other. From the dugout, Reeves and I watched them stumble and chase after missed balls.

"What's the report?" I asked.

Reeves flipped through a notepad.

"A fair amount of complaints. The key words that came up were 'tyrant,' 'pointless,' and 'impossible.'"

"Did they at least seem to find any joy in agreement over the situation?"

"Well, there was definitely a lot of agreement. I'm not so sure about joy."

We watched as one of the players missed what should have been an easy catch.

"They're not doing great, are they, Professor?"

"I guess it would be a mistake to bank on immediate results."

"What do you expect will speed things up?"

"The primary things that must be accepted to succeed in the face of a difficult change are urgency and vision. I fear right now these boys are lacking in both."

"Skill would probably help as well, Professor."

"Unfortunately, that will only come through practice, and practice is useless without motivation."

"I thought your speech about defeating Rodhelm was very motivating."

"It provided a carrot to dangle, but now that they're out there and actually having to experience the sweat and dirt of it all, I can't help but feel they will need some continued support."

"How should we go about that?"

"Reeves, I hope you remember our conversation on *Full Metal Jacket*."

....

It did not take long for Reeves to have the boys running laps around the diamond as he stood on the pitcher's mound, offering his words of encouragement.

"Do you think you have what it takes to win? Because from where I'm standing, it doesn't look like it! It doesn't look to me like you even want it! Like you even care one way or the other! From here, it doesn't look like you know the difference between baseball and rock-paper-scissors!"

I was surprised how gruff Reeves was able to make his usually soft voice become.

"The game with Rodhelm is this Saturday! Do you know what that means? That means we only have four days to become a baseball team! We only have four days to decide if we want to be winners or losers! You have to be intentional with every throw, every catch, every swing, and every step!"

He seemed to be doing an excellent job of establishing the *urgency* part of success. Now I just had to figure out the *vision* element.

"Do you call that running?! My grandmother can run faster than that, and she's in a coma! She missed my sister's wedding last summer! My second cousin's graduation! My father's retirement party!"

I decided this was the best time to relieve my assistant coach before things got too personal. I ran up from the dugout before he could get to his nephew's baptism. Reeves had a somewhat difficult childhood and I had no doubt he could pull from his family's experiences all day.

"Thank you, Reeves. I'll take over from here."

"I hope I primed them for you, sir."

"You were excellent."

Reeves went back to the dugout as I motioned for the players to stop running. They collapsed onto the ground in weariness as I approached.

"Good job, everybody. Let's take a few minutes and rest."

I motioned at Reeves to bring over some water. As he did so, I gave my next words further thought.

"Do you feel that right now? That iciness in your lungs? That's the Rubicon, the river you either cross or turn back from. Right now, everything in your body is telling you this was a mistake, but I know there's at least some part of your spirit telling you to keep going. Once you get past the pain, anything's possible, but that first hurdle; that's not an easy one to get over. If you want to cross it, you don't just have to want to win. You can't just do this to pass the semester. You have to do this because you believe in it. You have to believe it is worth it intrinsically, that there's a value to playing, that there's a reward in trying hard, in pushing yourself. I can give you the opportunity to prove yourselves against Rodhelm, but I can't force you to put in the effort it takes to make that opportunity worth it. That's on you."

I was surprised by the attentiveness and contemplation apparent on the faces of my players. However, I still knew there were a couple of steps missing if I really wanted to seal the deal; I had to give them some hands-on experience as baseball players, and I had to give them a taste of what they were after, a victory.

....

We had two more full days of practice. During this time, we rotated the players through different positions before assigning them their spots. This allowed the players a chance to get a sense of accountability and collaboration as they were gaining a better understanding of their teammates' positions. It also gave them a sense of initiative; they weren't just being assigned positions, they were figuring the plan out along with us and offering feedback.

I believed a quick scrimmage game would be a good way to boost morale. After a few drills in the morning, the "opposing" team arrived for the practice game.

The opposing team was made up of random students from around campus interested in a pizza voucher. No inquiries were made into their physical abilities or baseball experience. I wasn't looking for a good team, I was looking for an easy victory.

The game, as I stated, was to be a quick one, with only three innings as opposed to nine. I wanted to wrap up early and give the players a chance to rest before the real thing the next day.

....

The game went...unexpectedly. My plan to get a group of untrained individuals from around campus failed to account for one of them, Errol Sabini, being a high-school baseball champ. If it weren't for his temper, Errol could have gone to a much more prestigious university on an athletic scholarship. He threw away that chance when he assaulted an assistant coach.

I elected not to tell Reeves about this last part and instead just offered Errol a spot on the team then and there. He was so eager to play baseball again, he didn't even make any demands. I also decided to instruct Reeves to drop his drill sergeant act. Errol seemed in good spirits (and had been through court-appointed anger management classes), but I didn't want to take any chances. I still wonder if Errol would have made the cut on Shackleton's expedition. He could have benefited from better humility and people skills, but as clear as daylight, he was hungry.

The players were a bit down after losing the scrimmage game, but morale seemed lifted by Errol's addition to the team. I believe this still qualified as a short-term win. It also provided the rest of the team a sort of sub-leader to rally around. An oft-recommended step in leadership is to create "guiding teams," that is, leaders within the team who can better handle certain parts of the mission. Teams tend to do better when leadership is shared, rather than isolated by one dictator at the top.

In this case, Errol had given the other players someone who knew more about baseball than their coach. While I could act as their overall leader, he was our ringer, our specialist.

This also allowed us to adjust our strategy. All the rest of the team had to do was get on base, then let Errol bring them home.

After the game, when the team disbanded for the rest of the day, I went home with confidence. I left with a sense that, in spite of our inexperience and lack of preparation, we still had a shot at defeating Rodhelm. And, if Errol were to relapse, I had confidence that Reeves would be a fast healer.

to be continued…

Part 3:

The crowd in the bleachers consisted of the board of trustees as well as students from Saint Foy's and Rodhelm. The surprising turnout made me think that perhaps this game had inspired some degree of school spirit.

"Decent crowd, isn't it, Cal?"

I turned in surprise to see Dean Northum standing behind me, looking up at the bleachers, having somehow snuck up on me in the dugout as I watched my players warming up in the field with some drills.

"More than I thought would show up."

"They're mostly kids from Rodhelm, eager to see us receive a thrashing."

"I think they may leave pretty disappointed," I said, eying Errol Sabini on the field.

"I'm sure you have it figured out. That's what I told the board, in fact. I made sure to let them know that, even though we're a business school, the principles we teach have near-universal applications. They are well aware that your victory today will be nothing short of confirmation of your skills as a professor."

"Wouldn't that also imply then, that if I lose, my skills as a professor are lacking?"

"Hmm, I guess I hadn't thought of that. Well, it's no bother. I'm sure you'll still have your job after this."

He concluded his musings with a friendly, if a little too hard, slap on my back as he exited the dugout.

"Don't worry, Cal. I'm sure you'll do amazing."

I watched him return to the bleachers to schmooze with the board while I contemplated my career options. Said contemplation was interrupted by Reeves' arrival.

"Was that Dean Northum?"

"Just wishing us luck."

"Think we'll need it?"

"I think we'll need a miracle," I said looking at Sabini, "but fortunately, we've got one."

"Looks like the players from Rodhelm just showed up."

I exited the dugout to get a better view of the street. Sure enough, a bus had arrived. The opposing players got out and I could see that, like us, they had not exactly just stepped out of the majors. Their uniforms appeared second-hand and their physiques lacked almost as much athletic prowess as the majority of my players. This seemed less "David vs. Goliath" and more a wounded badger against another wounded badger, but with a good batter on his side...I feel I lost the metaphor somewhere.

"I think we're in pretty good shape so far," Reeves chimed in.

No sooner had he said this than the opposing team's coach stepped off the bus. I couldn't believe my eyes. There, among Rodhelm's team, the team sent here with the goal of humiliating me, stood Marion Crenshaw, my ex-flatmate.

....

My intention was to storm up to Marion with the appearance of righteous indignation, but after visibly catching my foot in a gopher hole and stumbling onto the road, I would have settled for the appearance of any dignity at all.

"Are you okay there, Cal?"

I opted to ignore Marion's question, unsure of its degree of sincerity or sarcasm.

"What are you doing here, Marion?"

"A few days ago, Dean Northum contacted Rodhelm about a baseball game. Wanting to make a good first impression, being new to the college and all, I volunteered to coach the team."

"So Rodhelm didn't even have a baseball team until earlier this week?" I asked hopefully.

"Oh, no. We've had one for years. The regular coach just caught a bad cold is all."

Perhaps I had eschewed the "David vs. Goliath" scenario too quickly.

. "Unlike Saint Foy's, of course," he snarked.

I've never been great at insults, so I elected to let actions speak louder than words instead of attempting a witty comeback.

"Our team may be new, but I think you will be quite surprised."

"Well, may the best man win," he replied, outstretching a hand.

I shook it before turning back to the field, walking away with a proud stride to let Marion see the confidence I had in the day.

Unfortunately, it is not easy to look confident when tripping on the same gopher hole twice in a row.

....

Henry Muldoon took to the pitcher's mound. I could tell right away that Marion and his assistant coach, a short fellow whose name I would later find out was Jared, were intimidated by his size. It soon turned out that the Rodhelm player up to bat had even more cause to be intimidated when a fastball shot off like a cannon into his left hip.

As the batter took his base, albeit with a slight limp, I made my way to the dugout to speak with Henry,

"You might be going a bit strong there."

"I thought that's why you wanted me to pitch?"

"Yes, but that strength doesn't do us any good if you hit the batter."

"I didn't like the way he was looking at me."

"And I don't like the way he just took first base, so how about we focus on the strike zone, huh?"

Henry played the rest of the inning much more gracefully, his pitches so fast that even when the ball made it into the strike zone, the batters were too scared of getting hit to swing straight. The top of the first inning ended without Rodhelm scoring a single run.

I was amazed to feel my heart beating out of excitement rather than anxiety.

....

Our team started the bottom of the inning in disappointing fashion, with the first two players up to bat striking out. My excitement had turned to disappointment. I was initially optimistic about getting a couple of players on base before Errol Sabini's turn, but at this point, I was just hoping to at least salvage *something* from this inning.

Errol walked to home plate, his stride that of a man on a mission. While the students from Saint Foy's either watched with concern or looked away in embarrassment, the ones from Rodhelm were smirking with confidence of a victory. The pitcher nodded at the catcher, pulled back for the throw, and fired a fastball, right down the middle.

Errol practically smashed the ball to the moon. No one on the opposing team had a prayer of catching that ball as it flew over the fence. The surprise was so great the audience could only watch in momentary silence...

...immediately followed by roaring applause (at least from Saint Foy's students) as Errol rounded the bases. We were back on the map. I was already thinking of what sort of smug speech I could deliver to Marion while completely disregarding anything I had ever heard about pride coming before a fall.

....

By the end of the third inning, Henry's arm had started tiring and it showed in his pitches.

The first batter to take the plate in the fourth inning was a small man, but more courageous than most of his teammates (and certainly more so than the ones Henry had struck out with fear on his side). The combination of his steadfast footing and tiny strike zone led to him taking first base.

Following him was another short batter. Henry attempted a lowball, but misjudged his aim and shot high enough that it was met with a bunt that got the batter to first.

The next Rodhelm player to come to home plate was about Henry's size and clearly not intimidated by the prospect of some forceful throws. With two players on base, a slugger at bat, and his throwing clearly past its peak, I wondered if Henry was the best choice to pitch.

Errol Sabini emerged as the most prominent candidate for his replacement. While not as physically strong as Henry, he had superior aim and could read the batter more clearly. I exchanged Henry for Errol and watched with clenched teeth as he took his first throw.

The behemoth at home plate swung harder than John Henry, striking nothing but air as a well-timed screwball landed in the catcher's mitt. My tension started to lower as Errol landed two sliders over the plate and struck out the batter.

As the audience cheered from the stands, I knew we had this one in the bag.

....

By the seventh-inning stretch, the score was eight to three, with us in the lead.

With victory all but assured, Errol, Reeves, and I decided to head over to the Rodhelm dugout for a gloating session (admittedly this was mostly my idea; Reeves advised against it).

"So, Marion, looks like the best man will win after all."

"Does he even go to your school?"

"I can show you his enrollment records if you'd like."

"That won't be necessary."

At this point, Jared the assistant coach made the mistake of chiming in.

"Might want to do a drug test though," he offered with half sarcasm.

"You accusing me of something?" Errol asked indignantly. "I'm clean as the day I was born."

"You ever see a baby right after they're born?" Jared replied with full sarcasm.

"I go to this school, and I'm not on anything. I swear on my mother's good conscience," Errol said, a fire starting to burn in his eyes.

"Then maybe we need to check your mother's repute," Jared snapped.

....

The events that immediately followed Jared's comment happened too quickly for me to fully make out, but they ended with him missing two incisors and the umpire kicking Errol out of the game, as well as a call to the police.

Reeves and I found ourselves back at our team's dugout, attempting to process the situation.

"You knew he had a temper when you brought him on, right, Professor?"

"I didn't think anyone would say something like that to him, Reeves. How could I have predicted that?"

"Isn't there anything in all those management books you read about dealing with unpredictable changes?"

"I believe I did recently deliver a lecture on leading in a crisis and adapting to change."

"Does this qualify?"

"As a change?"

"As a crisis?"

"Depends on how the next inning goes."

....

By the top of the ninth inning, our lead had narrowed to only one run and my players were clearly tired, both physically and emotionally, realizing the odds of keeping Rodhelm's team from taking the lead during their turn at bat were dwindling. I could see Marion's smug face from the dugout.

"He's mocking us, Reeves."

"We're still winning."

"Not by much. Not by enough, especially when our team is in the state they're in."

"You should still be proud of the job you've done, Professor. Who would have thought you could get a group of frisbee players this far?"

"I will admit pride in seeing them overcome their initial resistance; finding the right positions for them, the inspiration they got from seeing Sabini perform...I'm just worried they won't be able to weather this final storm. They seem too discouraged."

"Can you blame them, sir? They lost their best player."

"Perhaps it's time to review that 'crisis' lecture."

"Go on..."

"The first step is to admit we have a problem."

"So?"

"We have a problem."

"That's one down. Good progress so far."

"The second step is to learn. That means examining our situation and performance, as well as the causes that led to that situation. Before Errol was dismissed..."

"Wasn't he arrested?"

"Before he had to leave the game, we still weren't relying on him entirely. Henry Muldoon certainly had some luck pitching. This is the third step, to build on our advantages. We have to take stock of everything we have; all the resources at our disposal...Of course, it would be a mistake to look at Errol's contribution as purely athletic. He gave the team motivation and hope; things they are clearly now lacking."

"You suppose we need another miracle?"

"Not necessarily. Sometimes a small adjustment in the situation is all it takes to turn the tide. We also need to remind the team of why victory is so important and assure them they have what it takes it win."

"Should I try my drill sergeant routine again, sir?"

"At this point, I'm willing to try anything."

Reeves turned to the players, cleared his throat, and channeled his inner tyrant.

"What are you doing?" he yelled. "I see you sitting there warming the benches, moping like you just got turned down for prom! What kind of outfit is this? You see this ball?"

He grabbed a baseball.

"I want you to imagine this is your fear. This is your humiliation. This is your weakness!"

At that, he threw the ball out the dugout with enough force to put Henry Muldoon to shame. The air cracked like thunder as the pitch flew across the field. Even Marion's smug grin faded at the sight.

When Reeves turned back to the team, he caught sight of their faces agape and speechless. I managed to return to my senses enough to break the silence.

"Reeves! Where did you learn to do that?"

"I told you I had some experience with baseball, sir."

"You never told me you could throw like that."

"You told me you believed the best position for me was as your assistant coach."

"Reeves, part of building on your strengths means to look at your resources in a different light, to consider the alternative uses of those you lead and find where they are best suited to contribute."

"What does that mean, Professor?"

"That means that you're putting on a glove and heading for the pitcher's mound, Reeves!"

….

Nine pitches later and the game had ended, with our opposition unable to score even one more run. Reeves was carried off by the team on their shoulders and Marion returned to Rodhelm in defeat.

Dean Northum had come up to congratulate me, having sufficiently impressed the board of trustees who would no doubt accredit him with the victory. I chose not to be bitter, though, over this. It wasn't really my win either; it was the team's, and most importantly, Reeves'.

The high Northum was riding on would be ruined soon enough anyway when Jared's medical bill was delivered.

the end

Thriving in Change

My personal law of management, if not of life, is everything can look like a failure in the middle.
Rosabeth Moss Kanter

Key Principle: Help people to choose change

- At the team level, there will certainly be a variety of reactions to change, and at the individual level, we can expect a tug-of-war between excitement and anxiety. We dread the loss of comfort and certainty, but also lean into the possibility of improvement. Most people don't like this tension. We want to either accept change or reject it, rather than go through this internal battle.
- The leader's job is to help both themselves and their team choose to have a positive view of the change. Leaders want to make that happen as early as possible in the process and for as many people as they can. Our attitude toward change often has less to do with reality, and more with how we perceive the change as it develops.

Best Practice: Overcome Resistance

- Leaders serve others by taking the time to understand why people are unable to move forward, and then investing the time needed to support them through the change. Good leaders know that change is not just a command, but a process with multiple stages.

- In determining how to respond to resistance, leaders usually start by investing energy into educating their team about the change. We can't expect people to accept a new challenge unless they understand the change and its benefits. Sometimes all it takes is some information and a quick pep talk, but other times, people need to participate in the discussion and direction of the change. We all like feeling a sense of control over our lives when change occurs, even when so many factors are out of our hands.

- Often, even with more information and involvement, people still need support to navigate the change. This requires more training and more personal encouragement. A leader giving that extra level of close attention to each team member's development communicates a real desire to see everyone succeed.

Best Practice: Build Confidence

- Individuals, teams, and organizations need to believe in the reasons for change, the competence of their leader, and their ability to grow and contribute to the success of the transition. Confidence is a state of mind that reflects all the frailties and strengths of human nature.

- Some individuals enter the change process brimming with confidence, and others will feel like it will be yet another opportunity to experience the agony of defeat. Until we're convinced the change is both achievable and worth it, we are unlikely to try new things and take risks. Leaders need to design the initial experiences of change so they can provide support, feedback, and, most importantly, success.

- When we recruit selectively, we also greatly increase the likelihood of each individual and the team experiencing an initial win. While starting with the right people doesn't guarantee success, starting with the wrong people will certainly guarantee failure. There are a number of selection filters for determining the right people, with character, competency, and chemistry being the three most helpful general areas to shine a light on.

Best Practice: Gain Commitment

- Social norms and pressures play a powerful role in directing our attitudes and behaviors. Human nature leans toward moving with the group rather than traveling alone. Once a team, organization, or community fully commits to a direction and begins to align their behaviors, change becomes inevitable.
- In crafting a message of change, we need to first make sure it is easy to understand. People may not need all the details, but they do need to know the basics and what will be required of them. Secondly, the change must not seem too costly. If the primary focus is what will be lost, then people will lose their enthusiasm for the change. We can accomplish this by building on the skills and character qualities of those we lead. We need to reinforce the message that the organization or community has accomplished great things in the past. We have overcome significant obstacles before and know how to meet the challenge ahead.
- We want to shape the environment so people are more likely to lean into the change. This sounds like a huge task, but the good news is that the most effective modifications are often small tweaks. It turns out that

little things matter in how we respond. Often, leaders fall for the trap of thinking a big change only happens with bold, earth-shattering actions, but sometimes those big actions create even more resistance. Simple modifications that make it easier for us to make decisions, take action, and even believe that change is already creating benefits reduce the amount of physical, mental, and emotional energy required.

Reflection Questions

- When you hear the word "change," what is your first thought? What influences your reaction? What helps you to "choose change?"
- What approaches to overcoming resistance to change have you found most effective with yourself and in leading others?
- What is a short-term win you can pursue for yourself or your team that would create confidence in handling a current change?

Further Reading

Good to Great: Why Some Companies Make the Leap...and Others Don't, Jim Collins

Leading Change, John Kotter

The Tipping Point: How Little Things Can Make a Big Difference, Malcolm Gladwell

Confidence: How Winning Streaks and Losing Streaks Begin and End, Rosabeth Moss Kanter

The Ideal Team Player, Patrick Lencioni

Influencer: The Power to Change Anything, Joseph Grenny, Kerry Patterson, David Maxfield, Ron McMillan, and Al Switzler

Endurance: Shackleton's Incredible Voyage, Alfred Lansing

Reeves, the Middle Man

Prologue:
I shower every day. I brush my teeth thoroughly. I take vitamins and supplements. I even, on occasion, wear gloves when I go out in case I have to shake someone's hand. So, lying there in bed, with a 101-degree fever and a throat that was more phlegm than Adam's apple, you can imagine I was surprised.

I was also surprised to have Reeves serving me chicken noodle soup.

"Are you sure you don't want to at least see the campus nurse, sir?"

"We don't need to bother her, Reeves."

"I do wish you'd take this more seriously."

"Oh, it's nothing to worry about. I just need a little rest and I'll be all set to deliver today's lecture."

"You can't actually be thinking of going to class like this?"

"What other option do I have?"

"You could always just send your slides to the students along with some notes."

"Reeves, for the next three days, I have three lectures to give, all on communication. Now, what kind of picture am I painting of myself when I can't even properly deliver a message about communication of all things?"

"What's that adage you're always talking about? 'Focus on the receiver?' Right now, it feels like your focus is more on the sender."

"Well, I prefer to think it is because I am focused on the needs of my students that I want to give them the best experience possible, which means the lectures need to be delivered in person. Focusing on the receiver starts with empathy and understanding the needs of those you are trying to teach."

41

"Well, if it means that much to you for the lecture to be delivered in person, then why don't I do it?"

"You?"

"I know the material by heart. I'm the one who proofreads all your slides and notes."

Admittedly, Reeves was very familiar with the lessons. Part of what made him such an effective TA was his tenacity in listening to my lectures and his thoroughness in proofing my work. He was the best one could ask for in his ability to pick up on grammar and spelling issues. Unfortunately, he did not always pick up on the meanings of the sentences themselves. When I had first showed him today's lecture to proofread, "Customize Your Communication," he asked me if it was about cellphone plans.

"I don't know, Reeves."

"I won't let you down, sir."

"I have no doubt you'll give it your all. I just...don't want my students to think less of me. It is vital for a teacher to maintain appearances with his students if he wants to keep their trust."

"You're white as a mouse and sweating like a snowball in hell."

"That's a little harsh but I appreciate you not mincing words."

"You look like my Grandma Ethel."

"Is she the one..."

"The one in the coma, yes."

At this point, I *was* starting to wish he would mince words. The blame was on me for his recent, blunter attitude. I had made a rather mean-spirited comment toward him last week and, in an effort not to hurt his feelings, I told him I had only said it based on the principle of reciprocity. This is a communication approach based on influencing people by treating them the way we want them to treat us. I told him that I only spoke so forwardly because of my respect for him, as I wanted those who respected me to feel like they could be open with their feelings as well. As it turned out, Reeves had a great deal of respect for me.

"Of course, I must look rather sorry here in bed. I'll look much more like a professor when I'm dressed like one."

It was at this point that I threw off my blankets, marched to my dresser, and proceeded to change; dress pants, a fashionable coat, a catchy but not distracting tie, and I looked ready to take on the world.

"Sir?"

"Yes, Reeves?"

"You're aware you're still in bed, right?"

I looked down to realize I was still in my pajamas and had failed to even pull the blankets up. Maybe Reeves had a point.

to be continued...

Part 1:

Although Reeves had urged me to try and sleep, I decided to check in on the lecture's livestream on my laptop. It isn't that I lacked faith in him. It was more that I lacked faith in myself to prepare him appropriately. If anything, the fact that I only trusted myself to teach the class was a sign of humility.

The class was meant to be split into two parts; a lecture and then questions. The first part mainly involved a presentation of slides. Reeves methodically read from the speaker's notes, following the lesson plan to the letter. He was so dedicated to this task that his words came out stilted. He nervously tripped over them as he checked the slides and lesson notes over and over to make sure he only said what I had written.

I had admittedly been rather insistent on him following my notes, but now realized I had possibly been *too* insistent. It was because of this that the lecture portion of the class had gone on much longer than it was supposed to, especially with the amount of "ums" and "ers" he fit into his talk. Ultimately, class ended before anyone could even ask questions on the lesson.

He returned to the apartment; the look on his face a clear indicator that he knew there was much room for improvement.

"Professor Schuster, I...hope you slept well."

"Well, Reeves, I tried but unfortunately the livestream of your lecture gave me a bit of pause there."

"I'm sorry, sir. I tried to stick to your slides as verbatim as I could."

"I fear that might just be our problem. I made a mistake by asking you to stick to the wording so strongly."

His expression at this admission of fault showed his surprise at my words.

"Yes, Reeves, even I must admit when I've erred in my judgment. It is important to possess humility in these matters, so it is with great humility that I must admit I am better than you at this."

His surprise turned to confusion. I realized my statement required clarification.

"By this, I mean delivering my specific lectures. It is much easier to memorize and elocute your own words than someone else's."

"So, what are you suggesting?"

"Customization. We need to find a way to translate my ideas into your words, giving you a better shot at presenting them correctly."

"How shall we go about that, sir?"

"Let's look at the lecture you will need to deliver tomorrow."

I pulled up the slides on my laptop. Reeves looked over my shoulder at the computer screen.

"The lesson is on sales approaches. In this part, I go over the key behavioral types associated with the DISC classification, pioneered by William Moulton Marston. D for Dominant. I for Influencer. S for Steadfast. C for Compliant. Here's what I wrote: 'Our behavioral preferences influence how we like to communicate, get our work done, and even spend our free time. Dominant types can be rather aggressive as they are very task-oriented and like to win. They prefer to lead rather than follow. The Influencer types are a bit more charming as they are people-oriented and want to create an experience as opposed to just complete a task. The Steadfast ones are typically quiet; they greatly value harmony in all their relationships and enjoy helping others. Finally, we have the Compliant types who follow the rules, dig into the details, and usually prefer to work alone.'"

"Which of these do you think best describes you? Probably a D, I imagine."

"Why is that?"

"Well, you have a great deal of trust in your decisions. When other people make suggestions, you usually…"

He trailed off, starting to realize his comments might not leave the best impression. I was less angry at him and more disappointed that he saw me as quicker to correct others than consider they might be right.

"Which of these would you say describes me?" he asked.

He was clearly trying to change the subject. I figured I would have to revisit this line of thought later.

"Well, most people don't fit squarely into one, but instead demonstrate a combination. I'd say you are probably a C with strong S tendencies. You have a great reverence for the rules and look for opportunities to help others and seek harmony with your team through following them."

"Well thank you, Professor Schuster. That's very complimentary."

"But remember, Reeves, that every behavioral type comes with strengths as well as weaknesses. In today's lecture, you followed the notes I gave you to such an extent that it proved a limitation. Trying to please everyone, even if that includes me, can be an impediment to your own creativity. That is why it's important for you to figure out how you would explain these concepts in your own words."

"In what way? Where should I start?"

"Well, the first step is probably to focus on your audience. Delivering a lecture is similar to selling something. You need to get them thinking about what you want them thinking about. Ever worked a commission job?"

"I sold cookies for a school fundraiser in eighth grade."

"Close enough. When you were selling those cookies, your task was to plant an idea in your customers' heads; they need your product, and your product is worth whatever barrier they must overcome for it. In that case, the barrier was a financial one. You had to convince them that your cookies were more important than their money."

"What barrier do our students face? The school already has their money."

"With a lecture, it's about headspace. You have a room full of sleep-deprived college kids with a lot else going on; other classes, social obligations...They have access to more information than any generation before them and it's easy to feel a sense of overload. You need to convince them that the information you have is more important than whatever else is on their minds."

"What do you do when you feel like you aren't getting through to them?"

"Usually I just schedule a quiz; that way they have to pay attention."

"Isn't that sort of punitive, sir?"

"What do you mean?"

"I recall in an earlier lecture, you explaining Robert Cialdini's principle of 'liking,' that is, people are much more open to persuasion if they feel they have something in common with you."

"Well, then, what's your idea, Reeves? How do you plan to keep them attentive?"

"Maybe a humorous example?"

"Like what?"

"Well, what if instead of just listing the traits of each behavioral type, I used a comparison? Like, what if each of them was attempting to...say...win a football game? Their behavioral styles could define their play-types. For example, the D could be overly aggressive, making him an effective defensive player but struggle to get along with his team. Each behavioral type could provide pros and cons, perhaps with humorous consequences."

"You can't teach business through humor."

"Why not?"

"Business-minded people don't understand satire."

"What makes you think that?"

"You ever met a business student who watches *Parks and Recreation*?"

"Plenty of them."

"Have you ever met one who understands that Ron Swanson is meant to be a blowhard?"

"I see your point. Still, I think if I'm careful, and show some well-drawn illustrations, I can give a clear and concise lecture as to my meaning."

"Well, if you feel it's best, then that's what you should do."

"Really, sir? You have that much faith in me?"

"Considering today's lecture, I have nothing but confidence any change will be an improvement."

to be continued...

Part 2:

The second day. The second lecture. I was on pins and needles in anticipation. I eventually realized this discomfort was because I hadn't taken Tylenol yet that morning and soon felt slightly better, but still nervous about how Reeves would do.

Watching the livestream of the lecture, however, I not only felt my migraine stop growing; it waned. Again, this could have been the Tylenol, but Reeves was genuinely terrific. He made the lesson fully his own. His wording, his tone...Even the hastily drawn quality of his illustrations on how different behavioral types play football gave them a certain postmodern flair.

Although the camera angle only gave me a view of the back of the students' heads, I could tell that instead of shuffling in their seats or twiddling their pencils, they were legitimately paying attention to the lecture...

...and then came those unfortunate words, "Any questions?"

Reeves pointed at the first student to raise his hand.

"Reeves...er...sir...you went over how to determine our own behavioral types, but how do you gauge someone else's?"

Reeves paused, completely frozen. It is difficult to fully describe his expression, but if a loading screen could have a human face, it would look like his.

The student continued, "That would be useful to know, right? When trying to deal with another party?"

The loading screen apparently finished and Reeves, regretfully, attempted to answer the student's question.

"Probably during kickoff, at least in regard to gauging the entire team. For a player-by-player basis, you're going to have to watch their individual styles, although it is usually safe to assume the defensive line are Ds. The wide-receiver has to demonstrate C qualities as their position is based mainly on the positions of the opposing team. The quarterback is usually thought of as a D, which is fair, but also must be a bit of a C to be compliant with the position of the receiver and an I to influence and lead their team. They can't just throw it randomly and assume someone on their team will catch the ball."

As I stated earlier, I could not see the faces of the students, but I assume they were reminiscent of loading screens as well.

....

Roughly a half-hour later, Reeves was back in my room.

"I'm sorry, sir, I panicked."

"What was even your thought process there?"

"I had spent so much time developing the lecture; putting things in my own words, building out the football example, that I failed to consider what kind of questions might be asked. This was all I had to fall back on."

"Oh, Reeves..."

"I was hoping that the students' confirmation biases would fill in the blanks and assume it was just a metaphor and I really knew what I was talking about."

"I don't think that was quite the impact. I think the impact was more that you weren't listening to them."

"How is that?"

"Well, you didn't actually answer the questions. You were so focused on what you wanted to talk about, the football analogy you spent so much time preparing, that you just defaulted back to that. You needed to put yourself in the mindset of the student actually asking the question."

"I don't know what to say, Professor. Maybe I'm just not cut out for this."

I was about to chastise him for his errors, when I remembered his comment the previous day; that I seem like a D type because I am so quick to point out the flaws in others rather than admit fault in myself. Maybe he was on to something.

"Don't...Don't be so hard on yourself, Reeves. You did a great job with the lecture up until it came time for questions. I wouldn't worry so much."

"Really, sir?"

"I should have done more to prepare you for all that. For tomorrow's lecture, I earnestly believe you will get it right."

"That means the world to me, sir."

"It really shouldn't be too difficult, Reeves. It all comes down to preparedness and adaptability. When a student asks a question, they are assuming you will know the answer. You will almost always have the benefit of the doubt, so there's no reason to be nervous. Listen carefully and demonstrate empathy. If you do that, you'll usually find the clarification you're looking for."

"But what if they ask something I just don't know the answer to?"

"Deflection and deferment are your two greatest friends there. You can try rephrasing the question and asking it back to the room."

"The Socratic method?"

"Yes. Socrates was the master of making himself look smart through other people's knowledge. This method also adds an element of interactivity to the class, helping to keep the students more engaged. Remember, we aren't just supposed to be transferring information to the students, we want to teach them to think critically."

"What if they don't know the answer, either?"

"Then assign the research as homework. It's a great way to offset your own workload."

"Your experience is invaluable to me, sir."

"The most important thing to remember is, if you know the material well, it is unlikely you will get a question that stumps you. Whatever questions they have will be on the lecture you just gave them. That means the possible questions...and answers...are very limited. Now, tomorrow's lecture is titled, appropriately enough, 'Designing the Presentation.' The lesson is on delivering information in a convincing way. If you can figure out how to give the lecture correctly, then you'll already have the answers all sorted out. It's practically built-in."

"Where do you want to start?"

"I'll give the basic sense of how I wrote it out, then you can focus on putting it into your own words."

I stylistically cleared my throat before starting.

"Designing an effective presentation starts with knowing the purpose of said presentation and determining what you need to cover to meet the expectations of the audience. The goal may be to help them gain some understanding or to motivate them into action. You want to tell them everything they *need* to know, but not everything *you* know. The key is to be efficient. Don't go overboard. People can only handle so much information at one time. You need to identify the core message and keep in mind that people will only remember the main points."

"So how do you make sure they're engaged when you deliver those main points?"

"People want memorable stories and concrete examples that illustrate the idea. Stories help you connect with the audience and provide emotions to go with your data points and analysis. They will remember a well-told story a lot longer than a series of facts."

"Like examining the behavioral types of football players?"

Sarcasm is rarely used for self-deprecation, but Reeves found a way. I decided to change the subject.

"And then we get to the part you most struggle with, the Q and A."

Reeves let out a disheartened sigh.

"If you go into it with that attitude, Reeves, you're just setting yourself up for failure."

"I'm just worried that, even with everything you've taught me, even if I do all the legwork, I'm still just going to get nervous and freeze up at the first question."

"The key to that is owning the room. When a student asks something, don't just stand at the desk. If you physically freeze up, your mind will follow. Move toward the student. Be slow...

certainly deliberate; non-threatening but maintain good eye contact and make sure to move your hands around a bit. It'll make you seem more engaged. Another helpful tip is to repeat the question when it's asked. Students are often timid about asking questions and may not speak loud enough. Rephrasing the question in your own words is not only a good way of making sure everyone hears it, but another method of owning the room."

"That's not a bad thought. Now that I think about it, you often do that in *your* lectures, don't you?"

"It's a very useful tool. Another is to end on a positive note. It's always possible a student might ask something that'll trip you up. After you have answered two or three questions, it's time to start looking for the best one to go out on. When you get a particularly strong question, and by that I mean one that'll make you look good, answer it thoroughly, reinforce your main point, and end the class."

"What if there's still time left?"

"Padding, Reeves. You ever notice I usually spend the most time answering the final question in all my lectures?"

"I never really thought about it, but I suppose you do tend to do that."

"See, Reeves, it's all about having the right tricks up your sleeve."

"I always thought it was about the strength of the content itself?"

"Common mistake, Reeves, common mistake."

to be continued...

Part 3:

I had the livestream up on my laptop about a half-hour early. Although this would usually be a sign of distrust, I felt oddly calm about Reeves' upcoming lecture. He had put in the work, learned the material, and I had faith he would pull through.

Just to be safe, in case anything occurred to worsen my migraine, I thought I might take some preemptive Tylenol. My heart skipped a beat when I searched through the medicine cabinet to find I had completely exhausted my supply.

....

I picked up two bottles at the campus pharmacy, my fever turning the mundane errand into a trek Ernest Shackleton would hesitate to endure, when a hand tapped on my shoulder.

"Hello, Cal."

"Dean Northum, what brings you here?"

"Oh, just picking up a few things."

In his hand was a bag containing enough Xanax and Benzedrine to kill an elephant and bring it back to life.

"I see."

"Yes, this one's for my narcolepsy."

"And the other?"

"Insomnia."

"Sorry to hear that."

"Well, we all make do."

He eyed up my Tylenol.

"Something to get you through today's lecture?"

"Oh, actually..."

"Hey, I forgot to mention, I'll be in the audience today. I've got a report to fill out for the board of trustees, just making sure all the professors are doing their jobs right, figuring out who's necessary and who's replaceable. I hope that won't be a problem, Cal."

I think I was finally able to understand how Reeves felt upon his first question yesterday.

"Cal?"

"Oh, no, sir. That won't be a problem at all.

"Well, I'll see you then."

He left me in the pharmacy, pondering my job security. I felt I was in a lose-lose situation. If Reeves did a great job with the lecture, I was assuredly replaceable. If he failed, then I was incompetent in my use of him as my substitute. The only way to remedy this was to teach the class myself and hope my fever had gone down enough that I could perform a satisfactory job of it. It was then that I realized I was sweating buckets.

....

The lecture hall has two entrances, one at the main hallway, and one off to the side. Although students are allowed to use either one, the side hallway was usually barren of anyone but teachers who used it to reach the front of the room faster.

This provided Reeves and I with adequate privacy as we discussed our predicament.

"Sir, you're pale as a corpse."

"As long as he sits far enough away, Dean Northum won't notice that."

"He might notice your slurring."

"I'm not drunk."

"No, but you're speaking with a delay, like your mouth is half-asleep."

"I checked my temperature this morning, Reeves. My fever broke."

"Well, it has most certainly come back, sir. You shouldn't give a lecture if you're feeling this way. What's the question you always say to ask before presenting? 'What is your level of enthusiasm?'"

"I can assure you, Reeves, I'm very enthused!"

"I think this might be more anxiety than enthusiasm, sir. You seem like you can barely keep your eyes open."

It is true that at that moment I would probably have given just about anything for a nap. However, I still felt compelled to deliver the lecture.

"You always say that the proper conditions for delivering a presentation are enthusiastic motivation and comfort with your format. Right now, you have neither, sir."

"Reeves, it isn't the format I'm uncomfortable with, it's consciousness in general, but that doesn't change the fact my job is on the line."

"I'm sure if you just explain things to Dean Northum..."

"Reeves, Northum is a man with a one-track mind. If he has it in his head that I need to deliver that lecture to prove my worth, nothing will convince him otherwise, especially in the state I'm in with no time to prepare my argument. Perhaps I would have a chance on a normal day, when we could chat in his office, but when he's out on a task like this, he'll be too focused on the forest to see the trees."

"Didn't you give a lecture once on impromptu presentations? Having to deliver a convincing speech with little notice? This is the same principle, isn't it, sir?"

Perhaps he was onto something. What a hypocrite would I be if I failed to actually apply the lessons I taught my students to a real-world problem? I needed to convince Dean Northum of my innocence in the roughly ten minutes left before class started. I went over the principles of an impromptu presentation in my head, soon finding myself in a lounge chair in the main hallway.

I began to formulate a short but persuasive presentation that would have the dean in complete agreement with my decision. I knew not to waste valuable time by apologizing for not having more time to make my argument. I needed to state the problem clearly and move quickly to a solution that provided a clear benefit to the dean. I could share my passion for developing others and tell how a professor investing in me had led me to discover my career calling.

Perhaps I could add how seeing another student deliver the lecture would reinforce the principles of persuasion I taught the class in earlier lectures. I would then finish with a stirring statement about being inspired by the dean's vision to help each student reach their potential.

My mind was racing. It was all coming together. I just needed to make sure I provided the right structure around the problem, the solution, and the benefit. I could already see the dean nodding in agreement.

....

I awoke to the sound of the noon bell, the upholstery of my chair soaked in enough sweat to guarantee no one else would sit there for the rest of the day. As I regained my bearings, I realized I must have fallen unconscious on my way to see Dean Northum.

The noon bell! I had slept through the entire presentation. This was the end.

As thoughts of doom and gloom passed through my mind, along with an attempt to remember if I was on good enough terms with my second cousin to ask for a job at his carpet installation business, the lecture hall doors opened and the students walked out.

Their expressions showed a mix of intrigue and contentment. Their words further reflected the success of the lecture. I heard adjectives such as "riveting," "compelling," and even "inspiring." If I had better regained my senses, I am sure I would have felt choked up with pride for Reeves, instead of just choked up due to phlegm.

Dean Northum exited the room last.

"Professor Schuster, I wasn't expecting you to already be out here. I figured the teachers usually stayed behind until after all the students had left."

As consciousness returned to my body, I attempted to figure out what he was even talking about.

"Nonetheless, I really ought to apologize. I'm afraid my narcolepsy kicked in and I missed most of the lecture. All I caught was Reeves' introduction. I'm sure you must have done a splendid job afterward though. I heard nothing but positive comments from the students. Good work, Cal."

With a smile, he gave me one of his patented, slightly too hard pats to my back and walked off, his smile no doubt fading at the amount of my sweat now on his palm.

....

Although I had intended a proper congratulation for Reeves that day, my fever failed to properly break until that night. The following morning, I was up and in the kitchen, preparing pancakes and sausages for breakfast.

Reeves entered, still in his pajamas.

"I didn't think you'd be up this early, sir."

"I feel like a million, Reeves."

"Smells good."

"Hungry?"

"Wouldn't say no to a bite."

"Glad to hear that. This is your victory breakfast."

"Then I should definitely have a bite."

"You've earned it, pulling me out of perdition like that."

"I think that was mostly on Dean Northum's narcolepsy."

"Yes, but he was assured of my skills as a professor by hearing the kind remarks the students were making about *you*. I ascribe this win to you, Reeves, not to our dean's orexin deficiency."

"I was just repeating the information you taught me, sir."

"Yes, but putting it in your own words was what made this whole thing work. One of the core principles of effective communication is motivation, and it is so much easier to feel invested and deliver a quality presentation when it's your own words as opposed to another's. True servant leadership involves connecting with your audience. You aren't just there to present information; you're there to teach. Students can tell the difference, and they could tell that your primary motivation was to be there for them."

"I think my primary motivation was helping you keep your job, sir. You think they'd let me stick around if you were fired?"

"I'm sure you'd find a place here, Reeves. It would take some effort, no doubt, but I believe if you put in the work, you'd be more than capable."

"Of course, for this to work, there would have to be an opening. A professor here would have to lose his position. I suppose it would be an easier transition if it were a professor in a topic I'm already familiar with; a topic I've already been grading papers and tests in."

As he took a bite from one of the blueberry pancakes in front of him, the pride I felt in his recent success surely remained, though I wondered if he was just thinking out loud or if there was something more sinister going on behind his eyes.

Of course, it was impossible to really feel a threat from a kind soul like Reeves, especially when his would-be nefarious smile had blueberry smears.

the end

Communicating with Impact

Effective communication is 20% what you know and 80% how you feel about what you know.
Jim Rohn

Key Principle: Make the Most of the Opportunity

- Effective communication requires a mix of knowledge, skill, and charisma. Charisma is that intangible quality that draws our attention favorably toward someone. People are much more open to receiving information and ideas if they feel they have something in common with the other person. We appear more charismatic when the audience feels we're involved with them, rather than just transferring information to them. Asking questions and demonstrating empathy raise the engagement level in any communication.
- Successful communication requires knowing the receiver and the environment. Simply finding more powerful language or more vivid images may not be enough to make a difference if we don't take into account situational

factors. Effective communication means understanding yourself, your audience, and the context.

- Messages that affect us emotionally are more memorable and likely to encourage us to take action. We are drawn to messages and messengers that share our passions and convictions. This means that, as senders, we need to put ourselves in the mindset of our audience and ask, "What's in it for me?"

- Whether we desire to educate or persuade, we all want our communication to be memorable. Interestingly, two of the biggest challenges deal with knowledge, but from opposite perspectives. One challenge is information overload, which is experienced by receivers. There is simply too much information directed at people today and no one can be expected to retain all of it. The second challenge is experienced by the sender, which is when we know too much. We have too much information to share and are likely to forget that our audience is not necessarily on the same page. We can easily attempt to teach them more about a topic than they can retain, or give them information that is unlikely to build understanding and interest.

Best Practice: Focus on the Receiver

- To truly focus on the receiver and not on ourselves reflects our whole philosophy of leadership. When we use an "others-centered" or servant leadership approach, our default is always to first consider the fears, concerns, and hopes of those we serve. To bring the receiver to a place they have never been, a vision they have never seen, or a truth they have never considered, we have to meet them where they are right now. That means demonstrating empathy, asking questions, and active listening. Harvard business professor Clayton Christensen once put it this way: "Without a good question, a good answer has no place to go." A failure to listen can waste a good question and potentially damage the relationship.

- We all tend to focus on responding more than understanding. How often has someone been sharing a story or a problem, and before they have gotten to the end, your mind has already been racing with responses. Once we start formulating our reply, our attention is diverted away from our audience and onto ourselves. When we focus on the receiver, we are much more likely to think holistically about what is required to move from transmission of information to transformation of beliefs and actions.

Best Practice: Customize Your Communication

- As we gain a better understanding of the receiver and their context through various tools, we need to intentionally alter our communication approach to reflect that. Too often, we naturally choose a communication method that would be most appealing to us, and in doing so, fall for the trap of making ourselves the focus. Our message is much more easily received when we use the same communication preferences as our receiver.

- Often, the difference between successful and unsuccessful communication comes down to simple questions like "When?" or "Where?" We can spend hours crafting the perfect pitch, considering personal and cultural factors, and integrating the principles of persuasion, and still get rejected. Other times, with little thought and a simple request, we get a "Yes." In those cases, the difference-maker is primarily picking the right moment, the right location, the right medium, or even just avoiding the wrong words.

Best Practice: Present with Purpose

- An effective presentation begins and ends with understanding the audience and meeting their needs. Good presentations are made memorable when the speaker truly believes in the message and can reveal personal authenticity and passion. We need to ask what our motivation is regarding the audience. Do we want them to simply like us, become more knowledgeable, change behaviors, or share our passion? We have to look inward to answer these questions and properly motivate ourselves. Audiences can tell when a presenter is just "showing up." Effective speakers, on the other hand, are fueled by purpose and optimism.

- Like all our communication approaches, we need to invest in knowing our audience (e.g., have they already been introduced to the topic, or are we the first to explain it to them?) Building understanding and changing behaviors is a process, and knowing our audience helps us figure out where our presentation fits into that process.

- Being purposeful means determining what we need to cover to meet the expectations and needs of the audience. We want to tell them everything they *need* to know, but not everything *we* know. Don't go overboard. People can only handle so much information at one time and not everyone is likely to share your enthusiasm on the topic. We have to determine what they already know, and what they need to know to satisfy their interest and meet their immediate requirements.

Reflection Questions

- What are examples of information overload (when you are the receiver) and presenting too much information (when you are the sender)?

- What is a speech or lecture you recall as both memorable and persuasive? How did the communicator connect with you on a deeper level?
- Compare one of your best presentations with one that didn't go so well. What were the primary differences in your preparation, format, motivation, delivery, and the audience?

Further Reading

Made to Stick: Why Some Ideas Survive and Others Die, Dan and Chip Heath

Influence: The Psychology of Persuasion, Robert Cialdini

Humble Inquiry: The Gentle Art of Asking Instead of Telling, Edgar Schein

The Coaching Habit: Say Less, Ask More & Change the Way You Lead, Michael Bungay Stanier

The Last Lion: Winston Spenser Churchill Alone, William Manchester

Reeves Fights the Power

Prologue:
Reeves is a man of many hobbies. Over the course of this semester, he had found himself a member of athletic teams, Dungeons & Dragons groups, and a Dave Matthews cover band that each had an increasingly negative effect on my sleep schedule.

The good news was that over the last few days, he had found a new pastime that produced far less noise. The bad news is that I could only assume this change of pace would have an eventual negative result as whatever force had recently compelled my friend and TA's silence would be a force not to be trifled with.

The even worse news is that this thought served as an even harsher impediment to my sleep. I was nervous.

....

It was on a Sunday that I found myself laying on the couch by the billiards table, trying my luck at an afternoon nap after barely staying awake through a dry sermon at chapel that morning, hoping to recover the energy to finish my work on the week's lectures.

Then *she* knocked.

"Cal? Are you in there?"

The voice was unmistakably that of Jesse McNamara, no doubt here in her usual role as Dean Northum's harbinger of some slip-up that would trickle down to my neck of the woods. I considered staying silent, hoping she would go away, but curiosity got the better of me.

"Just give me a moment."

I opened the door, giving her a perhaps unfairly sudden view of my baggy eyes and weathered disposition. After taking in the sight with some mixture of pity and surprise, she entered the apartment as politely as possible.

"Hey, you doing alright, Cal?"

"Just hoping to use this weekend to catch up on some rest."

"About that..."

"I'm led to believe Dean Northum is not too fond of my plans?"

"Dean Northum has no problem with them. It's the teachers' union I'm here on behalf of."

The other cause for my nervousness, even more so than Reeves, was the announcement that the staff at Saint Foy's College would be receiving pay cuts across the board. Some were discussing the possibility of a strike.

"They're calling for a strike."

I guess it was more than just a possibility.

"What do you make of all this, Cal?"

My immediate thought was that a strike would mean not having to finish my lectures for the week. This brief moment of joy was interrupted when I remembered I had bills to pay.

"I suppose this was inevitable. I'm not sure what I can do about it, though."

"There *is* something..."

Her words were interrupted by Reeves exiting from his room, looking as nerve-racked as I was; eyes tired from excessive reading and shoes worn out from equally excessive pacing. Visible in his room were newly placed posters of Italian anarchists and French revolutionaries; all made in China.

"Good morning, comrade. I see management has made its way here."

"Management?" Jesse asked.

"It's one in the afternoon, Reeves."

"One, already? I must've been letting time get the best of me. I've got places to be!"

He hurriedly grabbed his jacket, draped over the billiards table, and rushed out the door.

"What's going on with him?" Jesse inquired.

"He's been reading theory."

"What theory?"

"Oh, I don't know. He started auditing a new class, something to do with European history, and the professor got to talking about...I'm not even sure; communism, socialism, distributism...some "ism." He's been holed up in his room ever since, living on a diet of manifestos and uncooked ramen."

"I supposed microwaves are too bourgeoise?"

"The humor is appreciated, but I'd rather get back to the teachers' union."

"Oh, right. Well, essentially, they need you to represent them."

"Why me?"

"Well, the dean likes you, for one."

"There has to be another teacher up to the task."

"The vote wasn't even close."

"If there was a vote, why wasn't I there?"

"They tried calling you yesterday."

It was then I remembered I had turned my phone off for the weekend in hopes of catching up on my sleep.

"Please, Cal. They're counting on you."

"Why are you on *their* side? You report directly to the dean."

"I want this resolved quickly, just like everyone else. The dean doesn't know what to do in this situation. He needs you to represent him just as much as the union does."

I was flattered to be wanted by so many people; to finally have my strengths in management and negotiation be recognized by my peers, but I still felt I needed to clear some things up.

"So, Dean Northum wants me to represent the administration to the union, and the union wants me to represent them to the administration?"

"That's right."

"And that isn't a conflict of interest?"

"That's the best part; you have no interest. Everyone knows that you would rather stay on the sidelines and let others sort this out. Your lack of care makes you perfectly unbiased."

I can't deny my morale took a slight hit at finding out the true cause for why I was being given this position. I had half a mind to turn it down when I realized this was the perfect way for me to show everyone that my lectures were not just me "talking the talk" per se. They say that those who can't, teach. This was my chance to prove them wrong. Not only could I show my compassion to the rest of the staff at Saint Foy's, I could also demonstrate my proficiency in the very same values I taught in my classes. This could be an inspiration to both the faculty and the student body of the college. This was my chance to step up to the plate...also, the sooner I resolved this, the sooner I could get some shut-eye.

to be continued...

Part 1:

"Down with the establishment!"

"Power to the workers!"

Such chants filled the air as I headed toward Dean Northum's office, passing by a crowd of protesting teachers and curious rubberneckers. Considering the strikers were university professors and not dockworkers in the fifties, I felt curious about why their defiance against the dean had taken this direction...

...then I saw who was leading the chants.

At the front of the crowd, directing them with anti-establishment slogans was Reeves, a picket sign in one hand and a megaphone in the other.

"No work until our raise! No more of our surplus value being drained by the academic elite!"

Much of the crowd watched him more unnerved than inspired, but a fair number seemed genuinely enthralled.

"Reeves? What are you doing? I thought you had somewhere to be?"

"Yeah. Here! Standing up for the proletariat masses."

"Reeves, you aren't even in the teachers' union."

"No, but I am a teacher's *assistant*. That means I have just as much right to stand up for the common man as anyone."

I was about to respond but figured the simplest way to get him off his soapbox was to resolve the strike with Dean Northum. I rubbed my eyes, longing to trade my setting for a bed and the chanting crowd for a white-noise machine, and headed inside.

....

The dean's office on the second floor offered a prime view of the protest. Dean Northum himself stood at the windows, watching the scene outside nervously.

"How long have they been out there?" I asked.

"There was a small group out there for about an hour, but things didn't *really* kick off until Reeves showed up. What's going on with that kid?"

"He's been reading theory."

"What are they assigning them these days, Marx?"

"Give it a week. He'll move onto something else. Don't worry."

"What about the professors? Even if he moves on, the seed has been planted. Look at them out there. They want my blood."

"You could try raising our salaries."

The dean stepped away from the windows and sat at his desk.

"That's just not in the budget."

"There must be some department you could get the money from."

"I suppose," he said, pulling a binder out of a desk drawer. "I've been looking over a few, but I'm not sure how well that'll turn out." He flipped through pages, looking for candidates for the chopping block.

"How about athletics?"

"That won't work. The board of trustees likes our baseball team too much."

"Whose idea was it to form that anyway?" he asked as he looked through the list some more before arriving at his next idea. "Arts. That's it! This is a business school. We don't need a theater department. What purpose does that serve?"

"I think it's meant to be a creative outlet."

"If they want to be creative, they should form start-ups."

"I don't think they'll take it too well."

"Are theater kids known for being dramatic?"

I was on far too little sleep to deal with this. I took the seat opposite Dean Northum and resisted the urge to doze off.

"We're in trouble, Cal. Simple as that."

"You're looking at this all wrong."

"How do you figure?"

"Conflict isn't inherently a negative thing. All organizations go through it. Conflict means progress. As organizations grow and meet new challenges, there will inevitably be different ideas on how best to move forward. Healthy disagreement is a sign of the strong passions people have for this college. Conflict can be a way to get the best ideas and stronger commitment from everyone."

"That sounds like a lecture."

"I'm kind of doing a test to see if my lectures have a real-world application."

"I don't doubt they do, but I question your point about this having such a bright side. I'm not sure if I'm seeing those positive effects right now."

"That's because we're still early on in the conflict. We're in what's called the "awareness" stage. This is where both sides are putting their energy into clarifying their position and what they want. Both sides are recognizing there are some strong disagreements that need to be resolved. Now, do you feel the union has made their demands clear?"

Before the dean could respond, a thrown shoe managed to slam against the window, prompting the two of us to look out at the crowd.

"Rise against the authority! Hold the line until the wages of man can reach the true value of his labor."

We spotted Reeves out there with only one shoe on, hopping around, shaking his picket sign.

"Well, I believe they want to be paid more. They've made that clear. I wish they wouldn't throw things at my window, though."

"They've established their position. Have you established yours?"

The dean opened the window.

"There is not enough in the budget..."

A second shoe interrupted him, fortunately a bit to his left. The dean quickly slammed the window shut.

"Reeves just threw another shoe at me!"

71

"Oh, don't worry. He wasn't aiming for you."

"How do you know?"

"You've seen him pitch. If he wanted to hit you, you'd have his size twelve imprinted on your forehead. He's just trying to get your heart racing."

Dean Northum sat back down, breath clearly heavier and brow beginning to sweat.

"It's working, Cal."

"Let's just consider this an example of...escalation. It's often easy to focus more on attacking the other side than finding a proper solution. Right now, it feels like they're attacking you."

"So that means there's an imbalance?"

"Yes."

"So, I need to attack them, next."

"No."

"I can get the campus police in here; horses, riot gear, teargas, tasers..."

"Our campus security consists of two former mall cops with mace."

"But they *do* have mace?"

"Going on the offensive will just result in further escalation and make reaching a solution more difficult. Let's just lay everything out and face facts; we simply need more money."

"We could try a fundraiser."

"I don't think we have time for that."

"What about raising tuition?"

"Students only come here because they can't afford anywhere else. Raise prices and they'll leave in droves."

"So what options are left?"

I mulled it over, distracted by the irate professors outside before reaching my solution.

"Endowment."

"What?"

"How about an endowment? That's how other universities do it; get a rich graduate to donate some money and name a building after them or something. Instead of just dividing the pie, we can expand it. The question is, are there any alumni out there smart enough to get rich, but dumb enough to give us some of their money for nothing more than a plaque and a tax break?"

The dean leaned back contemplatively. Suddenly, his eyes widened in revelation.

"Makepeace Cormier; class of 09. He's a millionaire."

"That's perfect; a student who took the university's lessons to heart and applied them in the world of business."

"He got a winning lottery ticket."

"Well...that's kind of an investment."

"Really?"

"In actuality, buying lottery tickets goes against every principle we have ever taught."

"Oh...So, what should we do?"

"We need to make him feel that he owes us for his success. This could be a challenge as his wealth doesn't exactly come from practicing Saint Foy's principles. He might not feel indebted to us."

"So, what's the trick?"

"Make him believe that he is."

to be continued...

73

Part 2:

When I was a child, chicken noodle soup was my go-to remedy for insomnia. As I sat in the kitchen, slurping my late-night snack, I found even the nostalgic treat was no match for my anxiety over the problem. While Dean Northum and I had succeeded in getting an appointment with Makepeace Cormier, I was still racking my brain trying to figure out how to convince him to give the university its much-needed endowment.

I could have sworn I was on the verge of a breakthrough when Reeves entered, one shoe missing from his feet, the other one, I suppose, retrieved after hitting the window.

"That was a rather lively show today, wasn't it, sir?"

"Reeves, do you have any idea how difficult things are for me right now?"

"No more difficult than the plight of the worker. Look what they have us reduced to," he said, pointing at his missing shoe. "It's gotten to the point where a man of the working class can't even hold on to his own shoes."

"Reeves, you are missing a shoe because you threw it into Dean Northum's office."

I reached under the table and produced his missing footwear.

"Here it is by the way."

Reeves took a seat at the table and put on the shoe.

"Thanks for grabbing that for me, Professor Schuster. How is the dean, anyway?"

"The dean is scared stiff after today's demonstration."

"Why would he be afraid of us?"

"Afraid of *you*, Reeves; not us...and it might have something to do with those shoes you threw at him."

"He's seen me pitch. He must know I wasn't trying to actually hit him."

"Reeves, Dean Northum is what we refer to as...overreactive."

"He's a pessimist?"

"Not a pessimist. A pessimist assumes something bad will always happen. An optimist assumes something good is more likely to occur. People like the dean eschew 'good' and 'bad' for 'best' and 'worst.' If things are to work out, they will always exceed anyone's wildest expectations. If they are to fail, then it will surely be a sign of nothing less than Armageddon. If a woman compliments his tie one day, she must be head-over-heels in love with him. If someone throws a shoe at his window, then there is assuredly a plot against his life."

"That's ridiculous."

"The dean is something of a ridiculous man."

"Oh, dear. If I had known that, I would have stuck with just chanting!"

"Even there, he assumes the worst."

"Maybe I should apologize."

"Will you end the chanting?"

"No."

"Then don't bother. His nerves won't be at rest until this whole matter is resolved."

"But, if the teachers' union were to get their raise, then the strike would end and so...would the...chanting."

Perhaps my most recent noodle slurp was too groggy. Reeves finished the sentence looking up and down my wrinkled face and baggy eyes, made likely even less dignified by drops of soup I had been too weary to wipe off.

"Sir, you have something on your face there."

"I'm aware."

I somehow mustered the energy to make use of a napkin and resume our conversation with at least a crumb of decency in appearance.

"To answer your point, there is simply no money for the raise. That's why the dean and I are heading to see a Saint Foy's alumnus tomorrow; a fellow by the name of Makepeace Cormier."

"How will that help?"

"Makepeace is a very rich man and we're hoping he will offer the school a generous endowment."

This flared up something fierce in Reeves.

"Oh, well, isn't that typical? Once the peasants rise up, the bourgeoise looks for help from his fellow oppressors."

"Please, Reeves, not now. I'm tired."

"So am I..." he exclaimed, standing up, "...tired of injustice!"

I answered his call to revolution with a sigh and another slurp of my soup. I didn't care if he saw me in a messy state. I was defiant to get some sleep that night!

....

With somewhere between ten to fifteen minutes of sleep in my system (a dearth I blamed on the stress this whole situation was causing me), I found myself in a car pulling into the driveway of a three-story mansion surrounded by the greenest grass this side of the Shire. I had been routinely nodding on and off throughout the drive, kept from a proper nap by Dean Northum's interruptions about how we should go about our proposal to Makepeace.

I had finally managed to get him to settle down and rest my eyes when the sound of a leaf blower tending to that exceptionally green grass startled me right back into the world of cruel, oppressive consciousness.

We had arrived.

....

Within five minutes, we were sitting on the most expensive couch I had ever rested on, sipping hot chocolate shipped straight from the Himalayas, all served by Makepeace's valet, Martinet.

"Are the refreshments to your liking, sirs?" Martinet asked.

"This is absolutely delicious," the dean responded.

Although I tended to take Northum's words with a grain of salt, this was undoubtably not hyperbole. The drink was almost tasty enough to make me appreciate being awake.

"Very good to hear. Your host will be arriving momentarily."

Martinet left us to our own devices, as well as to take in the impressive artwork lining the walls. The dean was the first to comment.

"He has expensive taste. What's that one over there? Monet?"

"Yes, right next to a print of the first issue of Spider-Man."

"Makepeace's tastes are certainly...eclectic."

I was thinking *"tacky"* but decided to keep my opinion to myself, instead opting to use our time more practically.

"This will be a peculiar battle; certainly uphill," I remarked.

"Why is that?"

"Clearly, Makepeace likes to put his money into flashy things, showy things...or things he can drink. A building named after him on campus will likely not seem worth his time."

"Then why even agree to meet us if not in good faith?"

"A kidnapper will agree to speak to a hostage negotiator, but that doesn't mean he intends to lower his demands."

"A kidnapper? Isn't that a bit extreme?"

I thought about the time I invited a former hostage negotiator to speak to a class, who explained that criminal and business negotiations are more alike than they would seem on the surface. He emphasized the importance of finding small, simple things that can move the situation toward a resolution. It is a mistake to only focus on the other party's stated demands, as opposed to their personal needs and wants. We needed to figure out Makepeace as a person, and not just as a potential source of money. This would make it much easier to use him as a potential source of money.

"Perhaps, but the rules of hostage negotiation are fairly universal. It's all based on the idea that each side has something of value to the other. Now, perhaps Makepeace thinks a building has potential in a way that could benefit him, or maybe he believes we have something else of value for him. His hostage is money, and we have to convince him to release it."

It occurred to me that usually it was the kidnappers trying to get money, not the negotiator, but I believe the point still stands.

"Hi," a voice greeted us from the opposite couch. We turned to see the source of the voice was Makepeace himself, reasonably muscular and clean-cut; eyes wide, but lacking much substance behind them. His clothes were surprisingly normal given the wealth on display throughout the mansion.

"When did you get in here?" Dean Northum inquired.

"Just now, when you were talking about hostages. What's that all about?"

I figured it would be best to change the subject.

"Cal Schuster. Pleased to meet you. I'm a professor at the college."

We shook hands.

"Makepeace Cormier..."

His expression shifted from polite glee to confusion as he looked at my hand.

"... and what are you hiding in here?"

At that, he pulled a string of candy out of my sleeve, the length of which must have been three or four feet long.

"I find candy necklaces are much better worn around the neck than the sleeve, Professor," he joked.

The dean and I stared at him dumbfounded before Makepeace chimed in.

"It's a magic trick!"

"Oh," I said, attempting to sound more impressed than annoyed.

"I'm working on becoming a stage magician," Makepeace explained.

"What a wonderful idea," said Dean Northum. "If there's one thing the world needs right now, it's more magic."

Makepeace extended a hand toward the dean.

"Good to meet you as well, Mister..."

"Northum. We met before, actually. I'm the dean at Saint Foy's. I shook your hand at your graduation."

"You'll have to pardon me. That seems like so long ago."

Thinking about the average financial state of a student at Saint Foy's, and then contrasting it to the opulence around us, I had no doubt that must have seemed like a completely different life to Makepeace.

"Anyway," the dean began, "regardless of the time passing, we're always happy to meet with our alumni. It is especially nice to see one getting along so well post-graduation."

Between a rather corny smile and the emphasis on Cormier's success, Northum was clearly laying it on thick. Makepeace, fortunately, did not seem to notice the artificiality of the performance.

"Hey, what kind of host am I?" Makepeace asked as he eagerly stood up. "I haven't offered you the tour yet."

"Actually, it might be best..." the dean began.

I interrupted him with an elbow jab to the side before commenting, "That sounds perfect. Lead the way."

As much as I would have preferred to keep the conversation on brass tacks and get this whole business over with, this was Makepeace's territory. It may have been our game, but it was his field. If we were to get what we wanted from him, we had to show a sign of good faith. In this case, that meant playing along with his ideas. This house tour would be nothing less than a chance to earn his favor and trust. It would also give me more time to work out how to make the proposal seem as mutually beneficial as possible.

....

What followed was a half-hour of looking around various expensive rooms, a forty-five-minute magic performance (Northum volunteered to be cut in half), two hours of watching *The Prestige*, and then twenty minutes of explaining the ending of *The Prestige* to Makepeace.

Finally, we found ourselves on the roof, sitting in beach chairs beside a swimming pool.

"Care for a dip?" Makepeace offered.

I know that earlier I had advocated for allowing him to lead things for a while, but after letting him do so for the past three-and-a-half-hours, I felt it was finally time for some initiative.

"Actually, I think now would be a good time to discuss our proposal."

"Oh, that's right," said Makepeace. "You said on the phone it was something about a building?"

"Correct," I began, "in particular, Jackson Hall."

"Oh, well I'm glad you thought of me, but I don't think I need a new building," he answered.

"No, it's not like that," Northum corrected. "You wouldn't be buying the building. This is kind of a fundraiser."

"But I thought Jackson Hall was already built. I could have sworn I debuted my magic act there, senior year."

"That's not the issue," the dean started before Makepeace interrupted.

"No, I remember it distinctly because that weasel Sebastian Cyrus sabotaged my act. We were both after the same girl that year and he kidnapped all my rabbits I needed for the show."

"The building *has* been built," the dean said, once again attempting to get Makepeace on our same page. "The money is for an endowment. See, in our current political climate, having a building on campus named after Andrew Jackson just won't do, Trail of Tears and such, so we've been looking to rename it, and who better to turn to for a name than one of our prestigious alumni?"

"Oh, so I give you money for a building that's already been built, and that I don't get; is that right?"

These words from most would have probably come across as sarcastic, but Makepeace legitimately seemed curious if this was what our proposal boiled down to. Although my first instinct was to correct him, I soon realized that, at the end of the day, this was essentially what an endowment was. Maybe Makepeace was slightly smarter than I had first thought. His next statement offered an explanation.

"I'm sorry. I'm flattered of course, but my accountant told me I shouldn't buy things I won't actually get to own after she found out about my NFT collection."

An accountant! When a rich man of a certain mental stature hires one, it's a coin flip whether they'll offer them some semblance of financial literacy, or railroad them for every penny they can take. It seemed Makepeace had lucked out on the former. I had to quickly offer some added incentive; something that included a financial buzzword or two to throw him off.

"This endowment, of course, will provide you with a generous tax break."

This seemed to perk him up.

"So, if I provide this endowment, then I'll get the money back from the IRS, right?" Makepeace asked.

"Is that how that works?" Dean Northum whispered to me.

"No," I answered to both of them, "the way it works is that, for whatever money you give us, you will not have to pay taxes on that particular sum."

"So, I would still be ultimately losing money on this?" Makepeace asked.

A moment of silence fell upon the room as Northum and I realized this wasn't working. We continued our efforts with him for a while but, ultimately, the topic always came back to him losing money on our proposal. We would have to look elsewhere for a solution.

....

Once more I found myself in my living room, this time with a budget report in front of me as I attempted to find an answer to the school's financial situation. Reeves exited his room, markedly less tenacious in spirit than usual.

"Something the matter, Reeves?" I asked.

"Oh, I don't know, sir. All the picketing and chanting and whatnot is fun but I'm starting to wonder if it's really getting us anywhere."

"I'm glad to see you're coming to your senses."

"I figured as long as the union was united, this would all be a piece of cake. Before the factory my dad worked at had a union, we were eating cold-cuts for Thanksgiving. After the union, we moved up to spam. I was hoping this would turn out just as well."

I was about to inquire into his sad upbringing when he noticed the papers in my lap.

"What's all this?"

"Budget reports. I'm trying to find something the dean might have missed; somewhere we can save money."

"Any luck?"

"I see a few spots where we might get a little here and there. Perhaps it could all add up, but I wouldn't count on it working out."

"Why's that, sir?"

"Both sides in this are too set in their ways. The union wants the administration to just magically pull all that money out of thin air, and the administration just wants the union to stop complaining and get back to work. It's like a line has been drawn in the sand. If the budget is going to be altered or the salaries raised at all, it will require a great deal of compromise that neither party is too excited over."

"What about that Makepeace Cormier fellow? Wasn't he how you were going to 'pull that money out of thin air?'"

"Unfortunately, that fell through. The negotiation proved to be a little one-sided."

"What do you mean?"

"Well, in a negotiation, the likelihood of an agreement exponentially increases when both sides have a greater incentive to find a mutual solution than to leave the bargaining table. If one side believes they are better off walking away, it is very difficult for the other side to convince them to keep negotiating. With Cormier, he could turn us down and be better off. "

"How so?"

"We brought nothing to the table."

"That is a little one-sided, I suppose."

"I guess that I'm exaggerating. From a practical standpoint, we were able to offer a tax break and his name on a building. It turned out neither was worth the effort to him. Neither felt as good as just keeping his money."

"So, what's the plan now?"

"Hope for a miracle."

"Is that practical?"

"No, but it's all we really have at the moment."

"Maybe the union and the administration will find a compromise. Perhaps Dean Northum will come through after all."

I appreciated the optimism, but a miracle honestly seemed more likely.

to be continued...

Part 3:

The candle that burns twice as bright burns half as long. Reeves acted as a sort of sugar rush to the teachers' union, and they were ready to crash. After all the marching and chanting, everyone was more than ready for the strike to end. Unfortunately, no one was ready to call it quits without a raise, but they were exhausted enough to agree to a sit-down.

We set the meeting for ten sharp.

....

The conference room, aptly enough on the second floor of Jackson Hall, held one table and twelve chairs, only four of which were necessary for today's meeting; two at one end for Dean Northum and Jesse McNamara, one in the middle for me, and finally, one at the other end for the union representative. I wondered who they would send.

"Who are they going to send?" asked the dean, apparently curious as well.

"Hess Bartleby," replied Jesse, glancing over a folder.

Unable to conjure the energy to do so for real, I let out a mental sigh at the name of Hess Bartleby. No more than a dozen words had probably been shared between us, and half of them were too vulgar for print; all from his side, of course. Remarkably, his attitude inspired few fights; something no doubt owed to his glasses, short stature, and balding head that clearly created a "lose-lose" situation for anyone involved with him in fisticuffs. No one wants to be known as the heel who beat up or *got* beat up by such a person.

....

Five minutes later, Hess entered the room, chewing gum, sat down at the end of the conference table, and gave us a glare that could burn a hole through concrete. I decided to break the tension with a casual opener.

"Hess, good to see you. I hope you slept well."

"Not a wink."

At that, he spat the gum into a trash can across the room. For around ten seconds, the rattle and hum of the waste bin was the only sound in the room until Dean Northum broke the silence.

"You should try melatonin; good for migraines too."

"I sleep better with my bills paid," Hess replied.

"Clearly, you want to start this right away," Jesse interjected before Northum could respond to Hess, "which I am entirely on board with. I only wished to ask, and I'm not complaining, but where's Reeves? Is there a reason he's not here with you?"

"Kid said he was busy; probably for the better. I don't know about you, but I don't need all that *theory* for this. What the teachers' union demands is simple; higher salaries."

"And the response of the university," Jesse replied, "is that there is simply not enough in the budget for so many raises."

"Without teachers, this isn't really a college."

"Well, without a college, you aren't really teachers."

I would normally feel content with Bartleby and McNamara having a snarky back-and-forth all day; means less work for me. The only problem was that this wasn't getting us anywhere. Snark is hardly a path to mutual gain.

Unintentionally, both had hit upon the key to the principle of mutual benefit. In this situation, the union's strike was hurting the school, which in turn was hurting the teachers. The two needed each other. Neither benefited from walking away.

Perhaps I could find a way to unite them through inanity; presenting a reflection of their counterproductive arguing.

"What a novel solution! A university without teachers, and teachers without a university. This could revolutionize the education system! Lower costs *and* higher quality!"

I was met with confused gazes. Maybe I needed to really hammer this home.

"This is the solution to all our problems. If both sides walk away, then everyone wins; the professors can teach without the school, and the university can save a great deal of money by not having to pay the professors. Everybody wins!"

After a moment to attempt to process my proposal, Hess offered his rebuttal, "That doesn't make a lick of sense. What are you talking about?"

"Yes," concurred Jesse, "I have to agree with Professor Bartleby. That makes no sense. If we don't get somewhere with this negotiation, then we all lose."

"You're a professor, Cal," began Hess, "I can't believe you would think *either* side walking away would be the best result, let alone *both*."

Now they were getting it. I had managed to get them to agree on a point, that walking away was a rather sorry option.

"You might have a point, both of you," I said. "I know tensions are somewhat high now, but it's important to remember that none of us are enemies. None of us are even really on different sides."

This last comment inspired a scoff from Bartleby and an eyeroll from Jesse. I decided to put aside their cynicism and continue.

"We all want what's best for the college. After all, we are all a part of it. The only difference here is that we can't all agree on what the best path forward is. How about we look at this as less an argument and more a discussion. What is best for Saint Foy's?"

"Better paid professors," said Hess.

"Snow cones in the cafeteria," said Northum.

The dean's response gave me a better idea why the school's budget was in dire straits. Maybe I could still salvage this.

"I think the dean raises an important point."

"Really?" asked Jesse, clearly not used to hearing such a statement.

"Maybe a percentage of the budget is being spent on unnecessary things that could help pay for higher salaries for the staff."

"But we haven't even bought the snow cone machines, yet."

"Dean Northum, please," I began, "let's remember my previous point. We're all in this for the best of the college. Is spending the school's shoe-string budget on snow cones really the answer?"

The dean hesitated, but eventually had to concede, "I suppose not...but I think the union should have to give up a few frivolities as well."

This was starting to get antagonistic again. I had to step in.

"Let's not look at it as your frivolities versus theirs. This is about finding things money is being spent on that do not provide the value that money is worth. We just need to consider some alternatives with the budget."

"Like what?" asked Hess.

The dean turned to Jesse for much-needed support. She looked over the budget folder in front of her before giving it.

"The university offers usage of several cars for members of the senior staff, as well as reimbursement for the teachers who use public transit to get to and from the school."

"If you get rid of those, how are we supposed to get to work?" Hess rebutted. "You want us all teaching from home?"

"No, but the union could organize a carpool system. That would save the university money on the cars as well as the bus passes that it could use on higher salaries."

"If that's the only way, fine...but the teachers driving those cars better get reimbursed for gas."

Jesse looked at the folder again.

"That's acceptable. Even with the added gas expense, it'll still be cheaper than the current system."

I mustered up a smile. Now we were getting somewhere!

....

Over the next half-hour, in pursuit of our common solution, we managed to nickel-and-dime the budget down to the point where the professors' salaries could be raised just enough to reach their demands. I could almost feel my head hitting the pillow already.

"Well," began Hess, "this wasn't quite how I expected things to go, but it seems to have worked out."

Dean Northum shifted in his seat, grumpy over the compromises but seemingly as ready to get this over with as any of us.

"For your side, maybe," the dean said.

Oh dear.

"What's that supposed to mean?" Hess asked. "You're getting your teachers back. That's what you wanted, right?"

"I wanted what was best for the university, not to strip it of every possible amenity. If this is the only way to get you to act like adults, then I guess it'll have to do."

"Act like adults?" said Hess, offended. "You were willing to put us out of work over snow cones."

That pillow suddenly seemed farther and farther away. I had to intervene.

"Hey, how about we just appreciate the value of compromise and..."

"Shut up, Cal," said Hess.

"You can't talk to a fellow professor like that," defended Northum.

"I'll talk to him how I please."

"If you use that kind of disrespect, then maybe it's time to reevaluate your contract with the university. That'll probably loosen up the budget a little."

"I have tenure...and if anyone's getting disrespected here, it's me, and if you're not going to respect us, then this negotiation's over. The union refuses to compromise on any of its *'frivolities.'*"

All this work, all this progress...just fell through my fingers in a flash. I could feel my throat getting dry. Hess stood up indignantly.

"If *you* ever grow up, then you know how to reach me!"

He exited, slamming the door behind him. I turned to Dean Northum, completely shaken.

"What just happened?"

He could only offer a shrug and concerned expression as response.

....

As though history was repeating itself, I once again found myself sitting across from the dean in his office, looking over the budget and attempting to drown out the protesting teachers outside, oddly enough absent of Reeves' voice.

"What are we supposed to do?" asked the dean.

"I'm at a loss. I can't believe things went from so right to so wrong in an instant. How did that even happen?"

"I'm scared, Cal."

I rubbed my eyes and sighed.

"What's wrong?"

"Just tired. Haven't had much sleep lately."

"Oh, why's that?"

I looked at Northum, at a loss for words at how someone in academia could be that dense, when a shoe struck the window.

"Oh, not again," the dean lamented as he got up to look.

Something out there caught his eye and his expression changed from frustrated to surprised.

"Hey, it's Reeves."

"I guessed that based on the shoe."

"And Makepeace is with him."

"What?"

I got up and joined him. Sure enough, Makepeace Cormier was out there with Reeves and the union. Reeves waved at the window, smiling and motioning us to come outside.

"Should we go out there?" the dean asked.

"What do we have to lose?"

"What if they throw more shoes at us?"

"I wouldn't worry about that. You're administration. I'm just a professor. They wouldn't do anything to me."

"But what about me?"

"I don't know. I guess you'll just have to roll the dice," I said as I headed out the door.

The dean soon followed, nervously.

....

We headed outside to find the teachers no longer chanting; no longer even angry. In fact, they all looked rather content. I turned to Reeves for an explanation.

"Reeves, what's going on? What's Makepeace doing here?"

"Makepeace," Reeves began, "why don't you tell them?"

He cleared his throat, doing his best to appear defiant.

"Reeves has been giving me a lesson on the plight of the working class. From my ivory tower, poisoned by the seductive life of the bourgeoise, I was unable to see what great oppression was happening all around me. It is because of this that I have decided to use my good fortune for the betterment of the proletariat, and offer the university an endowment to increase the salaries of its professors."

His speech inspired cheers from the teachers.

He leaned in toward Reeves and whispered, "Did I do that right?"

"Just perfect," Reeves replied.

As the crowd and Dean Northum started discussing the next step, I pulled Reeves aside for an explanation.

"What happened?"

"It's like Makepeace said, sir. I shared some elements of theory with him."

There's that word again.

"That's all?"

"Well, it was a start. I thought about a lecture you once gave, when you invited a hostage negotiator to speak to the class. He brought up how negotiations are really more about emotions than anything else."

"And that helped you convince him?"

"Makepeace kept mentioning an old rival of his, Sebastian Cyrus. I figured he must be a wealthy man to be on his mind so much and suggested we might try going to him next; offer to name the building after him for an endowment. At that possibility, he couldn't grab his checkbook fast enough."

"Well done, Reeves," I said, patting him on the shoulder. "Well done, indeed."

....

The rest of the week was marked by that greatest gift, sleep. The strike over, a raise in my salary, and a pillow under my head, I was able to finally catch up on my much-deserved rest.

After that, I figured I would head to the cafeteria for a snack. After some discussion with the dean, Makepeace had agreed to buy those snow cone machines after all.

the end

Creating Desirable Outcomes

Negotiation is the art of letting them have your way.
Daniele Vare

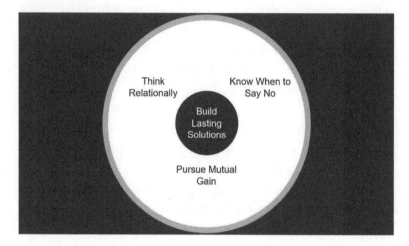

Key Principle: Build Lasting Solutions

- Conflict is not inherently a negative, but rather a needed element in high-performing teams. If a team is too harmonious, it is more likely to become static and non-responsive to needs created by a changing environment. This places leaders in the challenging position of determining when conflict is a positive presence and when it becomes a problem.

- The sooner we recognize the existence of differences in opinions, processes, and desires, the more likely we will be prepared for the possibility of conflict. We also must be aware of our own contribution to the presence of those differences, and how our responses will either lead to a solution or more dysfunction.

- Two common responses to encountering these differences are avoidance and escalation. Avoidance is often the preferred method in organizational and personal life; ignore the problem and hope it goes away on its own. This only works when the cost of addressing the issue is greater than the benefit of resolving it. Escalation brings the problem into the light where it can be dealt with. The challenge with escalation is similar to driving a car without brakes. We can't slow down when we need to, and we risk zooming right past the territory where a solution is possible. Escalation tends to result in people repeating the same arguments, using threats to force compliance, and forming coalitions.

- When we choose neither avoidance nor escalation, we are able to seek mutually beneficial and acceptable solutions. Both parties can appreciate their similarities, acknowledge their differences respectfully, and engage in constructive dialogue.

Best Practice: Think Relationally

- Effective negotiators always remember that relationships can either be a driver or a barrier to developing open communication with the other party. If we fail to establish a positive connection, we never get the opportunity for our most convincing arguments to be heard and accepted. Demonstrating humility, a desire to learn, and a genuine concern for the other person establishes a negotiating environment that fosters long-lasting solutions.

- We need to remember that people are emotional, and in order to solve the problem, those emotions will need to be addressed. The emotions may not seem rational to the other party, but they are a critical part of identifying a workable solution. By allowing the other side to vent their frustrations, as well as putting our own emotions on the table, we create more transparency. We can take our strong emotions like fear and anger and turn them toward solving the problem.

- Effective negotiators move the conversation toward each side's interests, as opposed to just their stated negotiating positions. Our tendency is to try to move the other side's position closer to ours, but analyzing the other party's interests will often show several possible solutions that could satisfy them. To determine interests, you need to demonstrate empathy and ask probing questions. Spending time discussing the problem rather than jumping into your proposed solution moves the conversation away from "positional" language like "This is what I am prepared to offer" to "interest" language like "This is what is needed for both of us to reach our goals."

Best Practice: Pursue Mutual Gain

- In negotiations, the lack of trust and the uncertainty of a common goal mean that communication is guarded. Disagreements are seen as negotiating tactics rather than coming from a genuine desire to sharpen ideas that can lead to breakthrough solutions. Creating an environment where effective brainstorming is possible starts by building trust if we want people to accept the vulnerability that comes with sharing their ideas. A common barrier to this is making people believe there is only a single correct answer, meaning their idea will probably be wrong. We also see creativity hampered when we assume resource levels are fixed; the pie can only be shared, not expanded.
- Pursuing mutual gain starts with a common understanding of the problem where both sides can express their issues and their passion for a solution. Next, we identify all the possible causes and barriers. It is also important to recognize that both sides don't have to agree with every item on the list. This is about encouraging collaboration as we acknowledge the variety of causes and stimulate the learning process. After considering the causes, we can start

identifying possible solutions. We want to demonstrate a broader range of thinking that goes beyond just our interests and addresses all the barriers that are impacting both sides. Ideas should be expressed tentatively, with a desire to make it easy for people to modify and improve them.

- Finally, we must decide if the group is ready for the final step of determining an action plan that can be implemented. We have to remember that a successful negotiation is not just about getting the contract signed, but what the agreement produces in the future. Ensuring both parties have the will and capability to fulfill their agreement needs to be integrated into the negotiation process. Building in a high level of accountability helps strengthen relationships as both parties demonstrate commitment to the agreement.

Best Practice: Know When to Say No

- We often find negotiations stressful because of the pressure to reach an agreement. External forces like organizational or community expectations drive us to consider options that are not beneficial to us. The pull of getting some deal, especially after a deep level of investment of time and emotions, can be such a strong motivator that we don't say "No" when we should. When we have already identified our options if we don't reach an agreement, we are better positioned to know when the other side's proposal is no longer favorable.

- You also want to determine the other side's options besides reaching an agreement. This often guides the scope of your offer and investment in the negotiating process. If the other side possesses very attractive options other than an agreement, you know they will have little incentive to work through difficult issues to produce a mutually beneficial solution. However, if both sides possess limited options, you can anticipate a greater willingness to find a compromise.

- Ending a negotiation or walking away from a conflict can also be a tempting solution when all the current options appear unfavorable, or when we perceive others are not valuing our ideas and feelings. However, if we walk away, we may miss the opportunity to create a pathway to a better situation for everyone involved. As we begin to engage in more direct dialogue or experiment with different solutions, we can test ideas and approaches and gradually implement the most workable elements. This enables us to keep our options open as we observe responses and results and defer making any commitments. In most situations, we will still arrive at a less-than-ideal point and will have to decide if we can live with the compromise. Sometimes, we have no choice but to walk away, but in others, through perseverance and creativity, we can bring about the needed change.

Reflection Questions

- What is the right level of conflict in your workplace? In your family?
- Do you tend to respond to conflict by avoiding or escalating? How does this impact you reaching the desired solution?
- How do you determine when you should continue to seek a resolution and when you should walk away from the negotiation?

Further Reading

Getting to Yes: Negotiating Agreement Without Giving In, William Ury and Roger Fisher

Crucial Conversations: Tools for Talking When Stakes Are High, Joseph Grenny, Ron McMillan, Al Switzler, and Kerry Patterson

Leading Quietly: The Unorthodox Guide to Doing the Right Thing, Joseph L. Badaracco

Team of Rivals: The Political Genius of Abraham Lincoln, Doris Kearns Goodwin

Reeves Takes a Vacation

Prologue:
The number nine bus was thankfully not crowded on the day I found myself on the road to Boston. Hess Bartleby, Reeves, and I had the back section almost entirely to ourselves. The amount of room allowed Hess the ability to sleep and Reeves to read a book he had picked up at the bus stop; something with a Greek letter in the title and a blurry man on the run on the cover.

"Nothing like a vacation to give one a chance to catch up on reading, is there, Professor?" Reeves asked.

"This isn't a vacation, Reeves," I replied. "It's a conference on bringing more businesses to the New England area."

I realized the irony in having the conference in Massachusetts, one of the parts of New England that was actually having no trouble attracting new businesses. Nonetheless, it proved a practical center point between the other states involved.

"It's a trip out of state to an all-expenses paid hotel stay. Even if it isn't a holiday on paper, I'm treating it as such."

While I appreciated Reeves' practicality of taking advantage of the benefits our trip awarded us, I couldn't help but feel he had gone a bit too far in his sunglasses and beach hat.

"I don't suppose you could have at least dressed for the weather?" I asked.

"As far as I'm concerned, this bus is taking us to Bermuda."

"You can't get to Bermuda from Massachusetts by bus, Reeves."

"Wasn't your last lecture on the importance of creative thinking; specifically about changing your perspective?"

While true, changing one's perspective is meant less to be about escaping reality and more about looking at it through a different point of view. I would have corrected him on this, but figured I would be better served saving my lectures for the conference.

....

A speedbump had been kind enough to save either me or Reeves the trouble of waking Hess shortly before we arrived at the hotel.

"I don't know why we had to take the bus," Hess complained as we entered the building. "If they want our participation, they should have come to us!"

I took in the lobby; a spacious, red-carpeted room with elevators and stairs leading to higher floors. A sign by the convention room signified where the conference was to take place. All around us were other convention attendees and hotel guests, as well as bellhops scrambling to get their bags.

"Isn't it nice to just appreciate the change in scenery?" Reeves chimed in as we walked toward the front desk. "It's been way too long since I've gotten this far away from campus."

We approached the desk where a clerk had just finished with another guest.

"Good afternoon, gentlemen. How can I help you?" he asked.

"We're here for the conference."

He eyed up Reeves, not exactly blending in with the other attendees in the lobby.

"Really?" he asked.

"Reservation; party of Schuster," I replied.

"Schuster..." he mumbled to himself as he looked through a desktop. "Ah, here we are. Rooms 803 and 804."

I had originally tried to get us each a separate room, but unfortunately the hotel was overbooked that weekend.

The clerk held up two keys before continuing, "803 is a double and 804 is the single."

The moment he let out the word "single," Hess dropped his bag and grabbed the key.

"I'll take that," he said, heading for the elevator.

"I guess we'll take the double," remarked Reeves.

"I guess so," I agreed, taking the remaining key from the clerk.

"As you can see, we're rather busy today, but I'm sure I can get you a bellhop for your bags if you'll just give me a moment," he offered politely.

"Thanks," I said, "but if it's all the same, we'll just take our bags up ourselves and save him the time."

"Whatever works for you, sir."

Reeves and I started toward the elevator when I turned to look at Hess' bag on the floor.

"Except for that one. Feel free to take your time bringing that up."

....

We soon arrived outside our room door.

"I hope you won't mind the lack of privacy too much, Reeves."

"Oh, don't worry, sir. I used to share a room with four brothers. To me, this is enough isolation to make Howard Hughes jealous."

Reeves entered the room first, quick to claim his bed, the one closest to the window, and started flipping channels on the TV.

"Come now, Reeves. We just got here."

"Just checking. It's not much of a vacation if they don't have HBO."

"Do try to take some notes, Reeves," I began, pulling my laptop out of my backpack. "This could be a very good learning opportunity for you."

"On what subject?"

"Well, how about we think back to the lecture topic we discussed on the way over here, creative thinking. While here, our team, being you, me, and Hess Bartleby, will have to put together a proposal for attracting new businesses to the state.

This will require a great deal of brainstorming and outside-the-box thinking."

I connected to the hotel Wi-Fi and started catching up on my emails. Reeves sat up.

"I'm sure if we hit a snag, one of the other teams will come up with the right strategy."

"Reeves, we are here representing Saint Foy's College to some of the most prominent business professors in New England. Why we were invited, I have no clue. Saint Foy's doesn't have the greatest reputation, but this is a chance to fix that, to prove our...worth..."

Reeves noticed me beginning to trail off.

"Something the matter, sir?"

"Just this email that came in. It's from the conference director."

"Anything wrong?"

"Probably not. Apparently, the team members of another university had to cancel save for one, so he'll be joining *our* team."

"That's good, right? It means a new perspective; more opportunity for outside-the-box thinking."

"I suppose. Let's see if they sent me any information on him."

My eyes widened in horror at the sight. Our new member would be coming to us from Rodhelm College. It was none other than my former flatmate, Marion Crenshaw.

to be continued...

Part 1:

There were around forty in attendance at the first conference meeting, not counting five or six people who had just entered to escape a rainstorm and were taking refuge at the concessions table in the back. Reeves was probably assumed by most in the room to be one of them as he enjoyed lady fingers and coffee while discussing his "beach read" with anyone who would listen.

Hess and I were sitting with a three-seat buffer between us as we watched Orson Somerville, the conference director, about my age with a shakiness to his speech and clear nervousness, at the front podium. He was addressing our reason for being there, aided by slide projections of charts and graphs.

"Over the past four years, New England has seen an eighteen percent increase in businesses leaving the area, in contrast to an only four percent increase in outside businesses coming in."

As he spoke, I eyed up the room, trying to find Marion to no avail.

"New England just doesn't offer the excitement and promise these industries are looking for," the speaker continued. "Instead, they are opting to go south to New York, or in an alarming number of cases, even further south to Florida."

I finally spotted him, up near the front and diligently appearing to take notes like the teacher's pet he always was. I would have been willing to bet, though, that half the page was nothing more than doodles and games of tic-tac-toe.

"We've been working with publicists, advertising agencies, and the Massachusetts Business Bureau, but what we really need now is *your* perspective; an educator's perspective."

I wondered what Marion was even doing here. Did he really care about attracting new businesses to the state? Was he just here for the ocean view?

As I tried to contemplate his reasons, my phone buzzed. When I checked it, I saw that not only had I neglected to delete

Marion as a contact, but that he had sent me a message – "Meet me at the coffee shop across the street when this is done."

....

To my surprise, Marion had not left me waiting. In fact, he was already sitting in a booth by the window, two cups of coffee on the table. I approached with something of a mix of curiosity and annoyance.

"It's good to see you, Cal. Coffee?" he asked.

I sat down and looked at the mug suspiciously.

"Look," he started. "I know we didn't end things too amicably last time, but we're stuck together. This wasn't my idea. It wasn't yours. Things happen. We just have to deal with it."

I took a sip from the cup.

"Cream, no sugar," I said.

"Just how I used to make it every morning."

"Yeah, Reeves hasn't quite figured out his way around the coffee machine, yet."

"Reeves, your TA? He's staying with you, now?"

"It's not like I could afford the place myself after you left. I was looking at cheaper apartments around town when he swooped in to save the day."

"I guess he has a habit of doing that, based on what happened at the baseball field at least."

I took another sip.

"Was that him by the concessions table back there?" he asked.

"I suppose he was kind of hard to miss."

"Is he back at the hotel?"

"No, he said he wanted to head to the beach."

Marion looked outside at the pouring rain.

"At least it won't be too crowded," he said. "So, who else is on the team?"

"Hess Bartleby."

Marion sighed.

"And I thought *our* reunion would be unpleasant."

"He's admittedly not in a great mood, but he does bring something to the table."

"What's that?"

"Impatience."

"And that's a good thing?"

"Let's call it...urgency. It's useful to have perspectives that balance each other. Reeves is in no hurry. To him, this is a vacation and he's more than happy to take his time with the project. Hess, on the other hand, wants nothing more than to get this over with and get back home. One of them brings urgency to the project, the other brings patience. Both are useful when you have a difficult problem that requires thinking outside-the-box."

"So, how do *we* balance each other?"

A volley of descriptors for Marion went through my head that I could contrast us with: *selfish, egotistical, conniving, disloyal...*

I, instead, settled on something less likely to start an argument.

"I suppose we also show two sides of patience. When you wanted a raise, you left for a higher-paying job. I just waited things out at Saint Foy's until the teachers' union could get one."

"Really? You managed to get a raise out of Dean Northum? I can't imagine that was easy."

"Yeah...you could say that."

"Wait a second. In this comparison, you're lining me up with Bartleby, aren't you?"

"Oh," I began, smiling, "I suppose when it comes to patience, you *are* somewhat comparable. I hadn't thought of that."

Maybe this wouldn't be so bad, after all.

....

Hess Bartleby, myself, and of course Marion, all found ourselves in my hotel room brainstorming our next step. As they sat on the beds, I leaned against the desk by the wall to address them.

"The first step in creative thinking is preparation. You cannot innovate without comprehension."

"Here he goes," said Hess, rolling his eyes and burying his face in his hands.

"I know this isn't exactly the fun part," I replied, "but if we are going to solve this problem, we need to understand it. We need to go through why so many businesses are leaving the area, but so few are coming in. Why is Maine less appealing than the competition?"

I turned to grab a folder from the desk.

"Now, the conference has provided us with these summaries of the situation..."

"So few are coming in," interrupted Hess, "because it's a dead state. Nothing of value comes from Maine."

Marion, with clear offense taken, turned to Hess.

"You can *not* say that about the state that brought the world such great minds as Joshua Chamberlain, Henry Wadsworth Longfellow, and Bette Davis."

Marion certainly had his issues, but at least his sense of pride extended to his state. Now I just had to figure out how to use that to generate some good ideas.

"Thank you, Marion," I said, opening the folder. "Now, according to this, the main issue is competition. When it comes to this part of the country, New York is the business center. People head south because taxes are lower in Texas, and it's cheaper to live in Florida."

A flash of lightning grabbed our attention.

"And it's a bit sunnier down there, too" I added.

"What about our culture?" asked Marion. "That has to have some appeal to outsiders. We have a great deal of history, of patriotism, and of prestigious institutions such as Bates College and the University of Maine."

"Unfortunately," I began, "according to this, decades of Stephen King novels have led people to primarily associate Maine with serial killers and alcoholics."

"There's got to be something positive in there," said Marion.
I thumbed through the folder.

"Lobster."

"That's it?" Marion asked.

"People like our lobster," I replied before setting down the folder. "At the end of the day though, what's the real problem? The primary obstacle for people? It's money. People have to be convinced they can make money here. Right now, they aren't. The other issues; weather, quality of life...Those come second. If they can make money, then they'll learn to adjust to the rest."

"What a revelation," said Hess, sarcastically, as he laid back.

Marion turned to me with uneasy eyes.

"I'm starting to remember why I left."

Before I could respond, the door dramatically burst open, Reeves on the other side, dripping wet in swim trunks with a similarly drenched novel in hand. Unsure what to say, we watched in silence as he walked to the bed, sat down beside Marion, and took a deep breath.

"Forgot my towel."

He looked around at the three men looking at him in confusion.

"How's the brainstorming going?" he asked before turning to Marion. "Have we met?"

"Marion," he replied.

Reeves extended a hand.

"Oh yeah, that's right. You used to teach at Saint Foy's, didn't you?"

Not taking the hand, Marion responded, "I don't think I left a minute too soon."

Clearly, we needed a break.

"Like I said, this is the preparation stage, where we gather information on the problem. The second stage is processing this information to come up with some ideas. I think we should take a reprieve; go off and work on something else until we get those ideas. It's actually very common to come up with answers to a problem when you're focused on something else. It's like when you can't remember something when you're trying to, but it comes back to you six hours later at random."

"So, we need a distraction," said Hess, sitting up. "What should we do?"

Reeves looked at each of us, no one offering an answer before he decided to opine, "We could go to the beach."

None of us decided to take him up on the suggestion.

to be continued…

Part 2:

A common barrier to creativity is ego; believing the answer to a problem can best be found in one's own head. While I certainly believe in the power of brainstorming, sometimes being trapped in a room with business professors is not the way to go when thinking outside-the-box is required.

It was this line of thinking that led to me and Marion Crenshaw standing in the bleachers at Fenway Park under two umbrellas.

"What are we even doing out here, Cal?"

Apparently, Marion did not fully agree with my line of thinking.

"I told you; we're trying to find inspiration from the city. Massachusetts has been doing better than Maine in terms of attracting businesses. Let's see if Boston will speak to us."

"Boston has much better landmarks to visit when it's raining than Fenway. Today's game was canceled for crying out loud!"

Admittedly, we were the only ones in the stadium; something I had initially viewed as a positive as it would give us a clearer environment in which to think, although the pouring rain proved a notable distraction. I still felt confident we could glean some inspiration from this place.

It was then, looking out at the rain-soaked field, imagining players fighting like their lives depended on it to score runs, that I decided to look back on baseball history for my answer.

"In 1935, close to fifty thousand people crowded this place with an estimated ten thousand turned away. That's sixty thousand people, in person, coming out here to watch the Sox take on the Yankees. That's more than this stadium had ever seen or would ever see again. What compelled that many people to do that?"

"1935? Was that the World Series game?"

"No. It wasn't. All they were fighting over was the number four spot in the league standings."

"Since when did you get so into baseball?"

"After our game last year, I started seeing the merits of the sport."

It was true. Our victory had inspired a further interest in the sport around campus. Saint Foy's hadn't suddenly become a baseball powerhouse, but the team stayed together. Reeves was, of course, still the best player.

Marion shrugged and looked off, shaking his head at the memory of his defeat.

"Okay, Cal, then you tell me. Why did so many people turn out for a game with such low stakes?"

"My theory? It's two-fold. The first part is that this was during the Great Depression. The people who had been laid off from work had nothing else to do, and the people with jobs needed the escapism. The second is that the Sox were the underdogs. They had been having a rough year and the Yankees were the clear favorites. The crowd came out because of hope; because they wanted front-row seats to David slinging a stone into Goliath's forehead."

"So...did they? Beat the Yankees that is?"

"Doesn't matter. The tickets were already sold. Now, this isn't exactly the Depression, but we aren't doing that great financially. Also, once again, the Yankees, so, New York, are causing us problems."

"The conditions *are* surprisingly similar," Marion begrudged. "So, the question is, how do we get the results to be similar as well?"

For that, I decided we should continue our tour.

....

Our next stop was the Bunker Hill Monument. Once again, Marion had some concerns.

"You just don't believe in the indoors, do you? The museum is right over there."

He pointed past the monolith to the Bunker Hill Museum across the street.

"That'll be too crowded to think in. Out here is where we'll find what we're looking for."

"I'd rather be in there looking at art than the B-level National Monument."

"Hey, this monument represents one of the most important battles of the Revolutionary War."

"Cal, we lost the battle of Bunker Hill. I'd rather visit the site of a victory than a defeat."

"There's your problem, Marion. You're looking at things too conventionally. It isn't all black and white. The British had the colonials outnumbered and their soldiers were better trained. By all accounts, it should have been an easy victory."

"So, how does this relate to creative thinking?"

"Let's say you're William Prescott, you're heading the troops, you're about to face a much stronger army, and your men are exhausted from setting up defenses all night. If you were going to have a prayer of winning, you would need to get creative."

"What was *his* strategy?"

"The first thing he had them do was build a dirt wall. They spent all night digging fortifications."

"Didn't you say that led to them being exhausted when the battle commenced?"

"Yes, but it provided cover. In an open-field battle, the winner is the side with the greater numbers. At least this gave them a chance."

"They still lost."

"But they showed the Brits they could put up a fight. This forced the Redcoats to reconsider their entire strategy. The losses they incurred at the battle showed them they could not just charge in and expect to win. They had to show a greater deal of patience and, at times, allow the colonials to retreat. It was this change in strategy that led to victory for the rebels when the Redcoats attacked New Jersey."

"So, you're saying that a loss can still have a positive outcome?"

"Yes. At the moment, it certainly seemed like pure defeat. Black-and-white thinking would only reinforce that belief, but examining the big picture shows that a loss can still lead to an even better result in the long-run."

"What's the positive result in all these businesses leaving Maine?"

"Unfortunately, that's where I'm still struggling."

"So all that, and you don't have an answer? You're just going to offer more questions?"

"Changing perspectives requires new questions to be asked."

"Well," began Marion, walking away, "I don't think William Prescott's perspective is exactly the key here."

I stayed behind for a few moments, looking up at the monument. The Battle of Bunker Hill and the Red Sox game of 1935 had shown that a defeat in battle or an economic crisis could lead to something positive. I felt sure that philosophy would hold the answer to the problem, but I just could not quite put my finger on it. Maybe Hess would have some ideas...

....

Marion and I arrived at Hess' hotel room. I knocked on the door and heard a groaning "come in" from Hess.

I opened the door, surprised to see Reeves, thankfully dry, in front of a whiteboard covered in text and pictures of various spots around Maine. Hess was sitting at the room's desk, thumping his head against it in boredom and frustration.

"Maybe we should come back another time," Marion opined.

Reeves turned to see us.

"Hey!" he said, excitedly. "Get in here. We were just brainstorming. We've been going over lots of ideas."

"Lots," echoed Hess in a cry for help.

"Well, that's good to hear," I said as Marion and I entered the room.

"Yeah," replied Reeves, "like, I was thinking about why people want to go places; uniqueness. What can Maine offer that can't be found elsewhere? Two capitals."

There was a moment of silence as we processed this suggestion, followed by Marion interjecting, "I'm going to my room."

He exited and I took a seat on the bed.

"So," I began, "How would that work?"

"When people set up a business in New York, they go to New York City. When they go to Florida, it's Miami. When it's here, they go to Boston. If Maine declares Portland as a separate capital, that means twice as many places where a business could be attracted to go!"

I turned from Reeves to Hess.

"Lots of ideas," Hess added, his cry for help now more a cry of defeat.

"Reeves," I started, "I appreciate the...creativity. I'm just not sure if that's the trick."

"Why not?" Reeves asked.

"Well...businesses tend to look for something serious. I'm worried adding a second capital would seem like too much of a novelty; a tourist trap. Also, New York City and Miami aren't the capitals of New York and Florida."

"Oh...I didn't know that," he replied, embarrassed.

"Hess, did you have any ideas?" I asked.

"Yeah," he started, reluctantly, "movies. Offer more tax credits to film and television production; give up on being the next Silicon Valley."

"That's not a...bad thought," I replied. "I'm a little curious about the logistics of this, however."

"That's not our problem," he said. "It's a good idea. It's something we can propose and then wrap things up nice and quickly."

"I'm not saying it's a bad idea. It might even be a good one. We just don't want to offer too simple of a solution."

"Occam's razor. The simplest solution is usually the right one."

"That's not...exactly what Occam's razor is."

"Why are you so opposed to this?"

"I'm not opposed to it. I'm opposed to black-and-white thinking. I'm against the idea that one solution must be the right one. The point of brainstorming is to offer ideas and discuss the details as a group."

"I'm not interested in brainstorming. I'm interested in getting this over with."

"But...we have to consider some of the inevitable questions that will come up. Why, for example, should people choose to film here instead of California. What do we have to offer?"

At this, Reeves slowly pointed at the whiteboard where the phrase "two capitals" was written. I started to think our solution wasn't going to be found in this hotel room.

to be continued...

Part 3:

I was nursing a ginger ale at the hotel bar when Orson Somerville entered. He took a seat nearby, dabbed his sweaty forehead with a breast pocket handkerchief, and waved the bartender over. He ordered a shot of something I had never heard of. I assumed it was probably stronger than my ginger ale as he set his eyeglasses down before having the drink.

"Hey there," I greeted.

He put his glasses back on to get a better look at me before responding, "Oh, hi. You're here for the conference, right?"

"Cal Schuster," I said, extending a hand.

"Orson Somerville," he replied, shaking it.

"So, what kind of ideas are people floating around?"

He sighed and turned back to the bar.

"Another one, please."

The bartender soon poured him a second drink.

"That bad?"

"I had a guy earlier recommend we should try convincing Disney to film the next *Star Wars* movie in Maine."

I wondered if that might have been...

"Of course, that was after he recommend naming Portland as a second capital."

Yep, that was Reeves.

The crash of thunder turned our attention to the window.

"Honestly," Orson began, "I don't know if anyone's ideas are going to be able to trump the turn-off of our weather."

"Maybe the next *Star Wars* will take place on a rain planet."

Orson chuckled.

"I guess I shouldn't be so dismissive," he began. "A good leader rewards risk. If someone pitches me a bad idea, but it's at least sincere, then maybe it's a step in the right direction."

"I don't know about *Star Wars*, but I did have a team member suggest trying to grow the film industry around New England."

"We've thought about that. Unfortunately, our geography isn't terribly unique. If people want an urban setting, they'd have an easier time filming in Los Angeles or New York. We've got some more rural areas here and there, but people are mostly using Canada for that. Turns out the only reason people will shoot a film in New England is if it takes place in New England. We're not...universal enough."

"Maybe we can use the weather for marketing? There have to be some CEOs out there who like rain."

This comment did not provoke the chuckle of the previous one, but at least encouraged a slight grin, possibly abetted by the alcohol in his system.

"We've just tried so many things," he began, his grin fading in dejection. "The state's poured a lot of money into this initiative."

"Thomas Watson, the man who founded IBM; he once said that 'the fastest way to succeed is to double your failure rate.' Keep trying ideas, even risky ones."

As I spoke, I realized I had been hypocritical in the brainstorming process. I had been so insistent on doing things my way; so dismissive of Marion's objection to our sightseeing tour and Reeves' two capitals idea. Admittedly, that last one wouldn't work, but maybe the thought process *behind* that idea had some merit that I just brushed off. I had been too scared of failure; of hitching my star to a bad idea that I had let my thinking become narrow. Perhaps I needed a kick in the pants to get back on track.

Maybe, I needed to give Reeves' approach a try...

....

A common barrier to creativity is the constant search for that "Aha!" moment; Paul's journey to Damascus, Archimedes' soak in the bathtub, Isaac Newton getting hit on the head with an apple...These are all instances where the great idea came to the person who needed it, but the catch is that none of them were in spots that would seem likely to produce such ideas. Paul did not find God in a temple, nor did Archimedes or Isaac Newton make their scientific breakthroughs in a laboratory.

It was this line of thinking that led me to the beach.

The sand was, of course, muddy. The tide was high and sweeping in a jungle of seaweed. Even the birds had abandoned the area. I stood there, soaking in the cold rain and watching the waves in the same clothes I had worn to the bar.

If anyone had been around, I would have probably worried I might look silly. Thankfully, these kinds of conditions ensure that only the foolhardy would be on the beach at this time.

"Professor Schuster?!" I heard from behind me.

I turned to see Reeves in swim trunks and a snorkel. In his hand was his soggy beach read.

My shivering body and chattering teeth prevented a lengthy or dignified response. Instead, I replied with a hand wave and a pained sound that approximated a "Hi."

"What are you doing out here, Professor? It's freezing!"

I managed to gather the strength to respond in full sentences, "I thought I might have been too dismissive of your ideas earlier. I figured I would come out here and gather some inspiration."

"I'm ecstatic you're here, sir, but are you sure you should be out in this weather?"

"You seem to be doing alright."

"Yes, but I'm in the prime of my life. You're liable to catch rheumatism!"

I thought about pointing out that you can't catch rheumatism; it's not a cold. However, I did not want to risk sounding overly critical and instead changed the subject, "Come on, Reeves, I can take it. I'm only ten years older than you."

"Thirteen."

Well, now *he* was getting overly critical.

"What have you been doing out here, anyway?"

"Oh, I finally finished my book."

He held up the paperback.

"That was fast."

"Well, there's not much else to do out here. I had to stop swimming when the lightning started up."

"*That's* where you draw the line?"

"I have to draw it somewhere. I have different strategies for different circumstances. When the ocean's all crazy and *black* like this, I stick to reading and sandcastles. When it calms down, gets a little color back, that's when I go swimming. That's more of my *blue* ocean strategy."

He looked out at the horizon to see the clouds beginning to part.

"Hey," he began, "I think the lightning's cleared up."

He quickly handed me the ball of wet pulp that was once a book and ran into the sea. I stood there, my brain sort of a static fuzz as I tried to process whether what he had said was asinine or brilliant. With Reeves, it was usually something of a mix of both.

This image, though, of the young man before me, enjoying his "blue ocean strategy," led me to an epiphany.

....

Once again in the coffee shop, this time with Orson Somerville as my company rather than Marion Crenshaw, I explained my new line of thinking.

"I was spending all this time trying to figure out how to grab established businesses, when I realized they aren't even the profile we need to be going after."

"They aren't?"

"No. Everyone else is already after them. We need a blue ocean strategy."

"What's that? That sounds familiar."

"It's the name of a book by W. Chan Kim and Renée Mauborgne. It refers to market space that's less sought after than the rest. Amazon isn't about to pack up and move their headquarters to New England. We need to be going after the *next* Amazon."

"Start-ups..."

"Exactly. Millennials aren't taken as seriously in the business world as well-established corporations. Let's say our marketing is aimed directly at them. The same goes for tax credits; make the incentive go toward newer businesses setting up shop here. We have the infrastructure. New England has its own Silicon Valley. It's admittedly not as big as the one in California, but that just means the barrier for entry is lower. Where is a new app-development company going to have an easier time making a splash, California or here?"

Orson sat back, musing over the idea.

"These businesses won't be bringing as much money into the state," he countered.

"Not at first, and many of them are going to fail," I began. "That's the nature of start-ups, but it's an angle we can offer that most states can't...and the ones that *do* succeed; they're going to make that much more of an impact."

He grinned.

"It's a better thought than most of what I've been hearing," he replied, leaning forward. "How'd you come up with this idea, anyway?"

The window rattled. We both turned to see the cause, Reeves with a large grin and completely soaked, tapping on the glass.

"Hey!" he yelled, "It's raining again!"

I turned back to Orson.

"Let's just say I have a muse."

the end

Delivering Innovative Solutions

The hallmark of a creative enterprise is the ability to generate effective surprise.
Jerome Bruner

Key Principle: Design an Intentional Process

- The creative process can often appear driven by sudden inspiration and reliant on a fair bit of luck. Unfortunately, innovation is more often a gradual process of development, experimentation, failure, learning, and eventually the beginning of an idea that just might work. Another seldomly true concept concerning innovation is the idea of the lone genius. Most of the innovations adding value to our lives today might have started with an individual asking the question "What if?" but would never have become a reality without a high degree of collaboration and encouragement from others. Innovation almost always requires deep learning and constant failing; only those who are truly passionate persist.

- Another misconception we often fall for is putting people into two camps: creative and uncreative. The process of innovation requires a multitude of skills and perspectives, allowing a broad range of personalities to contribute. Even if you feel like you are not the most creative person among your friends or colleagues, hopefully you will see there are many paths that can be taken to express creativity.

- Creativity begins with preparation. You cannot innovate without understanding. If you want a breakthrough, start with becoming knowledgeable about the subject. This is not usually the fun part of the process, but it is foundational and should not be overlooked. The next step is processing your ideas. Our brain often thinks most creatively when we aren't consciously focused on the topic. After a period of collecting information, we need to allow our brains time to make the new connections that are the basis of a creative idea. Revelation is the third part of the process, where the compelling, creative idea seems to suddenly come into view. Of course, we only see it because of the hard work of preparation and the time we've given ourselves to mull over different bits of information.

- Producing an idea is only worthwhile if it can be executed. Execution, the final step, is when the idea is brought to life in a tangible way that will produce a benefit. It requires hard work, investment, and the possibility of realizing your idea wasn't that great after all. This is why so many people settle for a revelation without completing the execution stage.

Best Practice: Change Your Perspective

- To think more creatively, we have to overcome our natural way of seeing things and be intentional in challenging our existing points of view and using new approaches. We can generate compelling questions when we reframe the accepted way things work. This requires us to move past the tendency to judge an idea or a situation before we really explore all the different perspectives. With complex problems, leaders who recognize the need for more learning and experimentation will prove more effective than ones overconfident in their one right answer.

- Perhaps the biggest challenge to creative thinking is overcoming our mind's fierce grasp of reality. It takes considerable effort to create an entirely new reality, and it takes optimism to consider changing what seems like an unchangeable situation. In more practical terms, thinking about what does not exist is likely the only way we have of eventually making it exist.

- Taking time to engage in creative thinking discussions and exercises will most likely slow down the decision-making process and lead to greater levels of uncertainty, at least initially. Over time, though, by forcing us to think more deeply, we will produce a much richer dialogue that will not only help us see more possibilities but also implement whatever solution is chosen.

Best Practice: Reward Risks and Encourage Persistence

- Einstein said, "It is not that I'm smart, it's just that I stay with the problems longer." No matter how smart you are, the most significant problems require deep and sustained effort. Too often, we surrender when a solution doesn't appear quickly. Leaders provide that vision and encouragement that keep us from quitting when something else looks easier.

- Leaders also have to reward risk. The greater uncertainty you have, the more focus you should place on learning, which means the greater likelihood of mistakes. Leaders model this by communicating they don't have all the answers and by empowering others to learn through taking action. Mistakes made by experimenting to test an idea or gain knowledge should be celebrated as moving the team forward.

Best Practice: Engage Everyone

- The foundation for a team or organization to generate and implement breakthrough ideas is a robust and varied flow of thought. This requires a community of thinkers capable of processing and refining the raw ideas. This provides the longer development period often needed for breakthrough ideas to survive and take hold. Finally, as we saw in the previous best practice, we need incentives for taking risks. Risks and rewards help individuals and communities prioritize the most important ideas for development.
- Organizations tend to do better when they invest more in a community-driven approach to generate ideas, rather than settle for the pursuit of a single idea. When communities are characterized by trust and diversity, there is a greater flow of ideas and shared learning. This reduces the risk of being paralyzed or confused by complexity as the community continually tests and experiments with new ideas.

Best Practice: Reflection Questions

- What are some of the barriers you have experienced to creative thinking and innovation? How have leaders in your life either helped you overcome these barriers or created them?
- What leadership behaviors are the most critical in developing a culture that encourages appropriate risk-taking and perseverance?

- What are some of the challenges you have noticed in looking at situations from different perspectives? How can you rediscover your curiosity?

Further Reading

Blue Ocean Strategy: How to Create Uncontested Market Space and Make Competition Irrelevant, W. Chan Kim and Renée Mauborgne

Loonshots: How to Nurture Crazy Ideas That Win Wars, Cure Diseases, and Transform Industries, Safi Bahcall

Age of Discovery: Navigating the Storms of Our New Renaissance, Ian Goldin and Chris Kutarna

Einstein: His Life and Universe, Leonardo da Vinci, Steve Jobs, Benjamin Franklin: An American Life, Walter Isaacson

6Ps of Essential Innovation: Create the Culture and Capabilities of a Resilient Innovation Organization, Michael McCathren

Reeves at the Crossroads

Prologue:

Fresh air, green grass, the warmth of sunlight offset by a cool breeze; summer was finally here. Having grown up in Maine, one might expect I would have developed a kind of Stockholm Syndrome sense of appreciation for our cold, rainy winters. Instead, all they had imparted on me was an increased feeling of relief when the sun finally came back out.

It was perfect weather for an outdoor graduation ceremony. A platform had been set up in the frisbee field along with a few rows of bleachers. A crowd of proud parents were seated in the stands watching their children come up, one-by-one, to receive their degree from Dean Northum.

Although not a parent, I was equally proud when my flatmate and TA, Reeves, stepped forward to get his degree, marking four years of hard work at Saint Foy's College.

Beside me sat Northum's assistant, Jesse McNamara, clapping as Reeves waved to us from the podium.

"Did his parents make it?" she asked.

"They're down in the front," I said, pointing at the couple a few rows down.

"You suppose they're surprised this day came?"

"Reeves may not be...traditionally academic, but, no, I doubt there was ever even a question."

"Really?"

"Maybe a small one."

....

Reeves had just scored his second strike, somehow unimpeded by his graduation robe and gown. I looked up at the scoreboard, realizing my chances of winning this game were essentially nil. I turned back to see Jesse getting a plate of nachos at the bowling alley concessions stand when Reeves tapped me on my shoulder.

"Your turn, sir."

I looked down the lane, weary of the task ahead of me.

"You know what, Reeves?" I began. "I think that getup might actually make you *better* at bowling."

I stood up and grabbed his cap.

"Let's even the odds."

He grinned as I walked up to the line, staring down the pins like we were about to draw pistols at dawn. I took my shot...and hit a gutter ball.

I handed the cap back to Reeves.

"Or maybe I'm just having some bad luck."

I managed to knock down three pins on my next roll. As Jesse took her turn, Reeves and I sat back to eat the nachos.

"Enjoy this while it lasts," I cautioned Reeves, "because once you start on your MBA, nights like these are going to seem pretty rare."

Reeves shifted, uncomfortable.

"What's going on?" I asked.

He gulped before speaking, "I was meaning to talk to you about that."

"About what? Your MBA?"

"I'm afraid I can't assuredly say I'll be here next semester."

I was stunned.

"You're giving up on your Master's degree, Reeves?"

"No. It's not that. I'm just considering getting it somewhere else."

"I thought you liked it here at Saint Foy's?"

"I do. Don't get me wrong...and that's exactly why I might stay after all. I'm just thinking about pursuing some other options. Saint Foy's is great for the Bachelor's program, but it isn't exactly the most...prestigious school."

I couldn't argue with that.

"I have nothing but respect for you and your classes, sir. It's just that...I keep in touch with my old high school classmates every now and then...see what they're up to; how they're doing. I was thinking about it the other day and realized...I'm the only one of us to go to college. Now I've got the chance to get an MBA, to really do something; get a proper career. I don't want to waste it."

I listened to him, speechless. This was the last thing I expected to hear tonight. McNamara's interruption only managed to partially snap me back to reality.

"You're up, Reeves," she said.

Reeves took one last bite of a chip before getting up to take his turn, leaving me to continue contemplating this situation. This could change everything. Every major event of my life at Saint Foy's this past year had been altered, usually for the better, by Reeves' involvement. Worst of all, I was going to need to find a new TA.

"Are you alright, Cal?" Jesse asked.

At that moment, an even more unsettling thought entered my head.

"I'm going to have to find a new flatmate."

to be continued...

Part 1:

Decision-making is at the core of every business principle: *Which company should I invest in? What product or service will do well in the marketplace? What amount of money do I put into marketing versus production?*

Uncertainty always lies at the heart of these questions, and yet, when I look back on the mistakes I've made throughout my life, the right decision seems rather obvious even though I did not always choose it. All the signs were pointing toward the internet overtaking physical media, but in 2007, when Netflix launched its streaming platform, I decided to buy stock in Blockbuster Video. At the time, the comparative successes of the two companies caused a great deal of uncertainty for me. Only in hindsight could I see that uncertainty removed.

As I sat in the living room, looking over my list of applicants to take Reeves' room (and more importantly, his share of the rent), I had a seemingly preternatural sense of foresight. Almost no uncertainty could be found...

I was absolutely certain I did not want any of these people living with me.

Among the "best" candidates were my old baseball recruits, Henry Muldoon and Geoffrey Catspin; fine outfielders, but poor company. I figured it was probably best to avoid living with a student again. Reeves was a case of lightning in a bottle.

As I was looking over the applications on my desk, I happened upon one of my lesson plans I had neglected to put away – a brief overview of the best practices of decision-making. I figured it was probably best to practice what I preach and so I took a look at my lecture on the importance of rationality.

While I didn't always do a good job of predicting the future, I prided myself that my business training had provided me with an analytical approach that allowed me to reach a logical conclusion. I needed to clearly define the problem, identify the most important factors, and then choose between the alternatives. My problem seemed obvious; I needed to find someone to take Reeves' room. The first step was to determine what was most important in selecting a flatmate.

This made me think that perhaps I needed to retrace my steps; figure out what led to Reeves living with me in the first place. The major factor was his predecessor leaving. Now that I thought about it, Reeves was practically the polar opposite of him as both a person and a flatmate. To find out what was necessary for his replacement, maybe I needed to go to the origin of it all...

I was going to have to talk with Marion Crenshaw.

....

In high school, I briefly held a job as a pizza delivery boy. The pay wasn't much but it gave me a good feel for the city. I hadn't been to the neighborhood Marion's apartment was in for the better part of twenty years, but I remembered it being covered in graffiti and litter.

It came as quite the shock when I drove into this part of town to find the liquor stores and smoke shops had been replaced with artisanal delis and overpriced coffee houses. What was happening to this city?

....

"Are you familiar with the 'broken windows' theory?" Marion asked, fixing a drink as I took a seat on his orthopedic couch. "It was introduced by social scientists James Wilson and George Kelling; a criminological theory based on the idea that visible signs of crime, even small ones like graffiti, encourage an environment of disorder. A neighborhood has a significant number of broken windows on account of vandalism. Perhaps someone sees these broken windows and decides this is a good area in which to commit a mugging. Small problems lead to big problems. The lesson? Little things matter."

He handed me a glass of club soda. His choice of drink was gin and vermouth.

"So, is that line of thinking what turned the neighborhood like this?" I asked.

"No. All the landlords just hiked the rent so the poor people had to leave."

"So, all that was just an excuse to talk about the last Malcolm Gladwell book you read?"

He took a seat across from me.

"One downside to living alone is not having someone to talk to about one's interests. For all the problems we had, we at least were into the same kinds of literature. It was like a live-in book club. I can't imagine your situation with Reeves offers that."

"Well, it turns out that might not even matter in the near future."

"What do you mean?"

"He's leaving Saint Foy's."

"Really?"

"Well...not necessarily, but that seems like the way he's leaning. He thinks he would be better off getting a degree from a more prestigious university."

"He's right. I can't blame him. Just as long as he doesn't start attending Rodhelm."

"I said a *more* prestigious university."

Marion offered me a sarcastic smile.

"So, what are your plans?" he asked.

"I'm going to have to find a new flatmate. That's actually why I came here. I'm reviewing applicants and none of them are clicking. I decided to prioritize my selection criteria by figuring out what made Reeves work. I'm trying to reflect on what influenced my decision. Do you remember my lecture on the importance of rationality?"

"So, where do I come in?"

"Reeves and you are at opposite ends of the spectrum when it comes to personality. I wanted to see if you could help me figure out exactly what traits I *shouldn't* look for."

"So, you came all the way out here just to tell me I was a bad flatmate?"

"It's more than that, Marion. I need to figure out exactly *why* you were a bad flatmate. Take a look at this," I said, handing him the applications.

"What's all this?"

"Potential replacements for Reeves. Which one looks the most appealing to you?"

He flipped through the pages for a minute before pulling one out.

"This would be my recommendation; Herman Wesker, the new accounting professor."

He handed me the page.

"Perfect," I replied before crumpling up the application and throwing it into the nearest trash receptacle.

"Now how about your second choice?" I inquired.

"Why don't I just pull out whoever I think is the worst pick and save us some trouble?" he asked sarcastically.

"Would you?" I asked, less sarcastically.

"Do you really think this poorly of me?"

"You're nursing a martini at eleven AM."

He put down the drink.

"We used to be friends, Cal. There was a time we got along famously."

"And then you left me to cover the rent myself so you could go to Rodhelm."

"Admittedly, we did not part amicably, but you tended to enjoy my company before that, didn't you?"

"Yes, but only because I had gotten used to you. Reeves vacuums. He cooks. He does laundry. He lets me know ahead of time if he's having friends over. I only saw you as the ideal flatmate until I saw what a quality living companion really was."

"Don't pretend this was all one-sided. You were the one who insisted on filling up half the living room with a pool table."

"That was for both of us."

"I don't even play pool!"

I rubbed my eyes in annoyance.

"Okay, so maybe our parting was inevitable. I would still like your help with this."

"You don't see the hypocrisy in this?"

"How am I a hypocrite?"

"You brought up your allegedly rational approach to selecting the best candidate, yet, you are ignoring another best practice you were always so fond of espousing in that particular lecture, 'learn at every step.' You can't just put together a list of what you do and do not like and insist your choice will fit every criterion. If that was the case, would you have even wound up with Reeves? No. He wasn't there because he fit some list; he was there because you were in need of a flatmate on short notice and he answered the call. You have to take risks; step outside your comfort zone."

I had to admit, albeit begrudgingly, that he was right. Reeves, on the surface, seemed like a terrible choice. He was good-natured certainly, but over-eager. I preferred to keep to myself; he was much more social. Not to mention we were not exactly intellectual equals. That isn't to say he wasn't smart, just that he wasn't quite...traditionally academic. Perhaps my issue was that I needed to be open to a nontraditional flatmate.

....

In the spirit of Marion's advice about taking risks, I decided to invite all the candidates, one-by-one, to interview for the room, rather than just selecting one or two who fit my strict standards and only talking to them.

First up was Herman Wesker, the aforementioned accounting professor. I had met him once before at a faculty party, although we did not talk for long. I prefer not to overstay my welcome at those sorts of events.

I welcomed him in at precisely three PM. My watch said it was 3:04, but he assured me he set his watch by the Navy Reserve clock. He was an accountant; I assumed he would probably be a little persnickety. I wasn't expecting him to show up looking like a relative had just died, however.

"Good to see you again, Herman," I said. "How's it going?"

"The market was up 1.6 percent," he began glumly. "My portfolio was only up by 1.3, so...I could be doing better."

Well... onto the next one.

....

Twenty-four hours later and I was in the faculty lounge, having gone through all the candidates, including the ones I would normally have not even considered, and sulking my troubles in a bagel.

Perhaps I had been overcomplicating things. Part of identifying one's influences involves acknowledging personal biases. We all have shortcuts we like to engage in when it comes to decision-making, and that is not inherently a bad thing. The initial shortcut I pursued was to eliminate candidates based on Marion's suggestions, only to decide to take the long path after all.

What if I went in the other direction? I hadn't been looking for a good enough shortcut in the first place. I had been trying to find the easiest way to replace Reeves. The most efficient shortcut wouldn't be that at all. It would simply be not to replace him.

I had to convince Reeves to stay.

to be continued...

Part 2:

I was dismayed at the sight of college brochures in the living room. I was even more dismayed to find out that Reeves was planning a trip to tour the campus of East Barrow University in upstate New York. I convinced him to let me tag along, warning him he might want me there to make sure he didn't get swindled by some fast-talking admissions counselor with a well-crafted emotional appeal. Decisions are too often driven by emotions and I needed time to develop my own emotionally persuasive argument.

It was around noon when we found ourselves in the school's central quad.

"The campus is pretty nice, isn't it, sir?" Reeves asked. "Cobblestone walkways. Brick buildings. Everything has a kind of classic, lived-in feel."

"Saint Foy's is lived-in," I replied. "Our buildings are *wonderfully* old. It's impossible to look at them without seeing their age."

I realized my sales pitch might have turned on itself a bit and decided to change gears upon seeing a coffee shop.

"I guess that lived-in feeling can't extend to everything. The shops look pretty new. Probably overpriced at that."

"Just for visitors. I think students get a pretty good discount."

"Student discounts are just code for overpriced tuition."

"Is that why Saint Foy's doesn't use them?"

Now that I thought about it, Saint Foy's had little in the way of student amenities. We barely had a cafeteria. I was worried drawing attention to this might serve to only further this school's appeal and tried changing subjects again.

"How about athletics? They have anything of note in that department?"

....

It was a practice day. A few minutes later and we were in the bleachers, watching EBU's baseball team showing more skill than any player to come out of Saint Foy's, with the possible exception of Reeves.

"I wonder when they have tryouts," Reeves pondered.

"You're too good for them."

"I doubt that, sir, but even if I was, would that be so bad? It seems like that would be a core element of leadership; to put myself in a group where my skills could raise the bar, rather than just look for easy victories. It's like your last lecture, the one on servant leadership."

It is true that every semester, after spending weeks teaching students how to think critically, communicate effectively, and make better decisions, I ended the course asking them to think about purpose. Too often it felt like students were more interested in knowing what would be on the final exam, but there were a few like Reeves who understood purpose was the most important aspect of leadership.

Although he had a valid point, Reeves had unintentionally given me a new angle.

"On the contrary, Reeves, the true exercise of servant leadership would be to stay at Saint Foy's."

"I'm not sure I understand, Professor."

"At Saint Foy's, you're easily the best player on the team, truly elevating them from mediocrity to decency. Here, you would just be making a good team even better. Who needs a doctor, the healthy or the sick?"

"Sir, I enjoy baseball, but I can't hang my hat on it, so to speak. This is like...What's that phrase you use when talking about decision-making? 'Prioritize your criteria.' My biggest goal here is getting my Master's to lead to a good career. Unless I'm planning to turn pro, which I'm not, that's what I have to prioritize."

He was using my own words against me! On one hand, this endlessly frustrated me. On the other, I was admittedly proud that he took my words to heart, even if his current application of them was working counter to my purposes.

"Reeves, in you I see a genuine servant leader; a leader who wants to add the most value to others. Where do you see the greater opportunity to do that, Saint Foy's or here? At Saint Foy's, you can be the star of the show, so to speak. Here, you risk just fitting in."

"There's a line in *Paradise Lost* like that."

Oh, good. He was appealing to John Milton. That man always had a sageness to his words.

"Something about ruling in Hell versus serving in Heaven. I think I'd rather serve than rule, especially if it means I go to Heaven."

And to think, I was the one who recommended that he read that book in the first place.

"Sir," Reeves began, "you make a good point, but I'm trying to think in the long-term here; both for the future and the past. The high school I went to…It made Saint Foy's look like Harvard. No computers, no textbooks less than a decade old. Half the kids were on food stamps. If back then I could look at myself now and see the opportunities that I have…I can't pass this up. I can't at least try to get into some schools like this. Who's to say I would even get accepted? It may be you're worrying over nothing!"

I took momentary comfort in his words, but they soon fell apart. Reeves wasn't the smartest kid at Saint Foy's, but he put in the effort like no one else. His grades were high and so were his extracurricular achievements. I had no doubt that he could get into a better school.

I sighed, almost in defeat. We watched the practice game continue for a few more minutes before I chimed in to suggest we grab a bite.

....

The cafeteria wasn't world class but it could certainly beat out Saint Foy's. We had Taco Tuesday; they had a taco bar open every day of the week. Their snow cone machine even had more flavors than ours.

As Reeves scarfed down a two-patty burger, a three-bean burrito, and a four-layer slice of cake, I went over my decision-making lectures in my head, looking for an argument he couldn't just bounce back and use against me, perhaps from a day he was absent.

I think it was his dessert that reminded me of the adage of having your cake and eating it, too. This was the practice of pursuing the "and."

"You know what, Reeves? I think we've failed to step back and consider all our options. We've been falling for the trap of feeling we must choose between two separate options. This isn't just a choice between Saint Foy's graduate program and a more prestigious one. There could be a third path that captures the advantages of both and is the best way to achieve your goal."

"How does that apply here?"

"Well, let's start with what you really want. Your whole reason for going to graduate school is so that after earning your degree, you can obtain a good teaching position, correct? You believe the more prestigious the university, the greater likelihood of that happening. But you also want to be in a place where you can serve, make a difference, and grow as a person. I know a place where a degree from Saint Foy's will be certain to land you a professorship."

He put down his fork, letting me know I had his full curiosity; a mighty compliment given how delicious the cake looked.

"It's Saint Foy's," I said with glee. "You can teach at Saint Foy's. I'm sure you could get a great position there after finishing your graduate degree."

He looked around, trying to find a momentary distraction in the room before sighing and returning his attention to me.

"Professor Schuster, was Saint Foy's the first university you tried to get a job at?" Reeves asked, embarrassed.

I could practically feel the color drain from my face.

"It's true, it wasn't my first choice of career. I...originally tried obtaining a position at a few different schools. I was young, fresh out of graduate school and all the most sought-after places were looking for someone with more experience."

"Oh..." said Reeves.

"But now that I have experience, and have even gotten some offers from other schools, I still choose to stay at Saint Foy's."

"You've had other offers?"

"A few...but I'm not leaving. Saint Foy's is my home. No, it doesn't pay that great, although things have improved some after the strike. I have *you* to thank for that."

He grinned.

"But I've gotten used to the way things work there. I know the rhythms...and most importantly, I have chances to help out; to do something great. Since being at Saint Foy's, I've gotten to start a baseball team. I've gotten to mediate a strike. You think I would have had those opportunities at an Ivy League school?"

"Do you believe I won't have the opportunity for greatness elsewhere?"

I started to feel trapped. Every argument I put forward had failed to make a clear-cut case for Saint Foy's and now I was stuck for sure. If I answered "Yes," it would show a lack of faith in him. Answering "No" would only validate his leaving. I finally decided to give up on this approach. It was time for honesty.

"I believe you will do great things no matter where you go. I just...don't want you to leave. I'm sorry, but that's all this essentially boils down to. You're the best flatmate I've ever had. There's never a dull moment! I know it's selfish, and after this, I won't keep trying to convince you to stay. I just...would prefer you continue your education at Saint Foy's."

Reeves looked down, and soon a bittersweet grin formed on his face.

"Thanks, sir."

to be continued...

Part 3:

Still unsure what Reeves' final decision was going to be, I once more returned to my favorite distraction from my problems, billiards. I was finishing a pickup game against myself when a knock came from the entrance.

"Anybody in?"

The surprise of hearing Marion's voice from behind the door led me to fumble my shot and land the eight ball in the right corner pocket. I set down the pool cue with a sigh.

"Come in. The door's unlocked."

Marion entered.

"You say that like I still don't have my old key."

"Oh, don't worry about that. I changed the lock months ago."

He looked at the billiards table.

"How's the game against yourself going?"

"I just lost."

"I guess that also means you just won, right?"

"Always the optimist," I offered sarcastically. "Need anything to drink?"

"Not really," he replied, leaning against the table.

We each waited for the other to speak before Marion finally broke the silence.

"Any news from Reeves?"

I shook my head and started setting up the balls for another game.

"Mind if I take a crack at this?" he asked.

"Really?"

"It seems like you tend to enjoy it."

"Do you know how to play?"

He grabbed a cue.

"I saw *The Color of Money*."

"What about *The Hustler*?"

"No, I skipped that one."

"You watched the sequel without seeing the first one?"

"The first one didn't have Tom Cruise," he said as he took his shot, amazingly missing the triangle of balls directly in front of him and landing the white one in a side pocket.

"Why don't you do that one over?" I said, putting the white ball back in place.

"Thanks," he replied before taking another shot, this one getting a couple of striped balls in. "I guess I'll be stripes."

"You didn't come all the way here just to play pool, did you?" I asked.

He took another shot, missing his intended target completely.

"Your turn," he said, stepping back from the table.

I prepared to take my shot when Marion chimed in, "Hess Bartleby's taking an early retirement."

"I hadn't heard about that."

"Yes, it was kind of last-minute."

"I wonder who's going to take his position."

I took my shot.

"I might."

I looked at Marion in confusion.

"What?"

He unsuccessfully attempted to hide the embarrassment on his face as he answered, unable to look me in the eye.

"Rodhelm let me go."

"That...surprises me. My issues with you as a flatmate notwithstanding, you're a good professor."

"It wasn't really anything to do with my ability to teach. It's all budget problems. A lot of good professors are having to leave."

"And you're going after Hess Bartleby's old job?"

"I was thinking of at least applying for it."

I wasn't sure how to respond. Part of me wanted to rub this in his face. My mind was filling with snarky comments on him losing his job. Looking at his disposition, however, I oddly enough lost the motivation to do so. Instead, I asked myself how Reeves would respond in this situation.

"Well...good luck."

He was clearly taken aback by the remark. I could see him analyzing my words in his head, trying to determine if they were sarcastic.

"Thanks," he replied, apparently accepting their sincerity. "I appreciate that."

I took another shot, missing.

"You're up."

He got into position and took his turn. I wasn't sure, but his demeanor almost seemed to convey...humility, although he was definitely attempting to cover it up.

Upon missing his next shot, this proved very difficult to hide.

....

My next stop was Dean Northum's office. He was going to be out of state for most of the summer and I thought discussing *his* leaving would take my mind off Reeves' leaving.

"It was a fine ceremony, wasn't it?" Northum asked as he sorted through a mess of papers on his desk.

"I think it went over quite well. Good weather for it, certainly."

"Reeves definitely seemed quite glad when I handed him his degree. I know it was hard to see from the stands, but he was smiling from ear to ear."

"Don't worry. I could tell from there."

Northum set down a stack of files in mild frustration.

"I thought Jesse took care of most of this?" I asked.

"Ordinarily she does, but I decided to give her a bit of a reprieve for a change."

"There is no greater act of leadership than to serve."

"Right you are, Cal. Right you are."

He looked over a form.

"Is it day, then month, then year...or does the month come first?"

"You...want any help organizing all this?"

"Oh, don't waste your time on my problems. The semester's over. You should be out enjoying yourself. I imagine that's what Reeves is up to."

I leaned back in my chair and suppressed a sigh.

"Did I hit a nerve?" Northum asked.

"Reeves is probably going to be pursuing his Master's degree at a different university.

"Why's that?"

"He believes it will lead to a better job."

"So, he's just going to leave you in the dust, then?"

"It's his choice. If he wants to do this, then I wish him nothing but good fortune. I'll get by."

"Glad to hear you taking on a positive attitude about all this. I know you two are somewhat close."

"Maybe it won't be too bad. One of the schools he's considering is only a few hours away. We can still visit every now and then...just won't quite be the same."

"Well, you're a smart man, Cal. It's like you said, you'll get by. I'm sure of it."

My phone buzzed. I checked to see a message from Reeves, saying he wanted to meet back at the apartment.

"Hey, I need to head out."

I stood up and headed for the door.

"Enjoy your summer, Cal."

"Thank you. I hope you enjoy yours."

....

Back at the apartment, I found Reeves preparing dinner. He had just stuck a casserole in the oven when I walked in.

"Smells good," I said.

"Thanks. I figured I've been making myself so scarce lately it would only be right to fix something special tonight."

I closed the door.

"So, you wanted to talk about something?" I asked tensely.

"Yes, sir. It's about me leaving. I've made a decision, actually."

I readied myself for the worst.

"I'm not going to pursue my Master's at EBU"

My eyes widened in shock. He made sure to chime in before too much relief could wash over me.

"I'm not going to pursue my Master's anywhere; here *or* at another school."

"But Reeves, I thought teaching was your dream?"

"It is...and that's why I'm heading back home. I'm going to teach at my old high school."

I took a seat, processing what he had just told me.

"I was thinking about your lessons on servant leadership, and I realized this was where I could best both serve *and* lead."

"What about all that talk you gave me about if your teenage self could see you now?"

"In a way, I'm doing this for him...for students like him at least," he said, sitting beside me. "Good teachers made all the difference in my life back then, and I'd like to do the same. This is where I can make the most difference; more so than at any university."

"You might have a point there."

"It just seems to make the most sense, based on everything you've taught me."

I was choked up, hearing how my lessons had encouraged him to take on such a selfless task.

"When would this start?"

"Next semester. September. I'll head over there in early August though. That gives us about two more months."

I grinned.

"Then let's make the most of it, Reeves."

....

The two months went by quickly, but they still hold a great deal of meaning for me. When all was said and done, we found ourselves at the bus stop.

"So, when does Marion move back in?" Reeves asked.

"Next week."

"Think it'll work out this time?"

"He's started taking a liking to pool. That's a good sign."

He chuckled. Admittedly, my time with Reeves had probably prepared me for living with Marion again. He had set a positive example of servant leadership that I could refer back to when in conflict with my prodigal flatmate.

"You sure you have everything?" I asked, feeling like a father about to send his kid out to school on his own for the first time.

"Relax. Anything I left behind, you can mail me."

"I suppose..."

A PA announcement for the bus arriving interrupted me.

"That's me!" Reeves said excitedly.

We loaded his bags onto the bus and he stepped toward the door.

"I'll miss you, Reeves."

"You know I'll miss you too, sir. Be sure to call every now and then. I might have passed your courses, but I imagine I'll still need your advice from time to time on how to handle the classroom."

"I will."

We shook hands, and then he looked back at the bus.

"Hey, I should probably get going."

"Yes, I guess you should."

He stepped on board.

"Reeves..."

He turned back.

"I'm proud to have worked with you. You've made me a better teacher and a better leader. Thank you."

He appeared to have a lump in his throat before offering a bittersweet smile.

"You too, sir."

The End

Discovering Opportunities in Every Decision

In the middle of difficulty lies opportunity.
Albert Einstein

Key Principle: Create Space for Understanding

- Effective leaders naturally consider how others will be impacted by their decisions. They factor in potential positive and negative reactions as people interpret the decision through their own perspectives. Leaders also must recognize that their own experiences and biases can prove to be significant obstacles to seeing situations clearly and making the right decisions.

- There are numerous places even in a rational decision-making process where we can disagree with team members. It usually begins with how we state the problem. Where you start plays a large role in where you finish. Without spending time agreeing on our problem definition, we are likely to see our purposes differently, as well as the scope of the problem itself. We also place separate values on different outcomes and resources, often due to having different information, objectives, and experiences. We can strongly argue our position from a very logical foundation but be in complete disagreement with our team and ultimately offer the wrong solution.

- Staying humble may be the most important principle in decision-making. It leads us to listen more, look more honestly at what drives our decisions, and maintain a healthy respect for all the things we can't control. Perhaps most importantly, humility allows us to be open to new information and ask the all-important question "Is it possible I could be wrong about this?" A good decision-making approach allows us to create space for richer dialogue where better decisions are made, understood, and implemented.

Best Practice: Identify Your Influences

- Our influences relate to our natural responses and subconsciously factor into our decision-making process. They can provide an advantage at times, but can also frequently be the primary drivers of our misguided decisions. Our behavioral preferences play a significant role in how we view risks, the pace of decision-making, and the desirability of outcomes.

- We also need to understand our brain's preference to engage in decision-making shortcuts, when that works to our advantage, and when it does not. Because it takes more energy to carefully analyze our situation, we often default to the simplest formula with the fewest variables. Using less information overall can make it easier to focus on only the important factors and more easily identify the problem. However, only having such a narrow view of the available data can lead us to misread situations based on biases or overlook critical information.

- Most experienced leaders take pride in being able to read people and make decisions based on intuition. It takes humility to step back and ask "What am I missing?", to withhold judgment, and to ask for help. Reflecting on past events and lessons learned will also make you more likely to differentiate between valid and invalid causes.

Best Practice: Learn at Every Step

- Decision-making is most often not a one-time analytical exercise yielding a final answer, but rather a process of designing experiments moving us in the right direction. Our most important decisions seldom offer a quick, obvious choice. We can make the mistake of relying too much on the past to predict the future. In more uncertain situations, experimentation is the only way to address the unknowns head-on.

- Once again, we see the importance of humility in applying a best practice. Sometimes leaders are impressed with their own intelligence which leads to overconfidence. However, often people are just overwhelmed with system complexity and complications. It becomes hard to differentiate between critical and inconsequential. We feel the pressure to make progress, especially in environments that value squeezing time and costs. We also want to see our ideas contribute to solutions but don't always respond well to criticism of them that could lead to improvement. The result is a failure to prioritize learning in decision-making.

Best Practice: Pursue the "And"

- When facing a decision, we have been conditioned to narrow our options and select the best one. Sometimes this is the best approach, but too often leads to missing a great choice for the sake of a mediocre one. When faced with two unsatisfying paths, if we think deeply enough, we can often identify a third one that captures the desired benefits of the other two.

- A key starting point in the process is to see that the goal of decision-making is about more than just analyzing options, but generating new possibilities. A unique aspect of the integrative thinking methodology is to articulate two opposing models. We tend to quickly gravitate to narrowing options that reinforce our existing preferences. By developing two opposing solutions, we force ourselves to think differently. Once both models are well understood and appreciated, we can see the similarities and differences between the models and, most importantly, what we prioritize in each.

- A final change in perspective to consider is "leveraging your disadvantages." When we only see how to use our most obvious strengths, we can get drawn into just considering one path. Sometimes we choose not to compete because we think we can only win if we excel in the traditional approach. Many of the great upsets in war, sports, and business occurred because the perceived weaker party chose an unconventional approach that neutralized the other side's advantages.

- Integrative thinking starts with how we view the problem, other people, other organizations, and ourselves. The more broadly we see each of these, the more likely we will discover multiple components that can be integrated into a better solution.

Reflection Questions

- How do you ensure you are making a rational, objective decision? What barriers do you have to be vigilant of to overcome?

- Describe a situation where you made a quick decision that proved correct. How were you able to make that decision?

Describe a situation where you made a quick decision that proved incorrect. What caused the error in your thinking?

- Describe a situation where you or your team faced a difficult situation requiring you to choose between two competing solutions where neither provided everything you desired. How did you reach a decision?

Further Reading

Thinking Fast and Slow, Daniel Kahneman

Blink: The Power of Thinking without Thinking, Talking to Strangers: What We Should Know About the People We Don't Know, Malcolm Gladwell

Just Start: Take Action, Embrace Uncertainty, Create the Future, Leonard A. Schlesinger, Charles F. Kiefer, and Paul B. Brown

The Opposable Mind: How Successful Leaders Win Through Integrative Thinking, Roger Martin

Creating Great Choices: A Leader's Guide to Integrative Thinking, Roger Martin and Jennifer Riel

Think Like a Rocket Scientist: Simple Strategies You Can Use to Make Giant Leaps in Work and Life, Ozan Varol

A Final Word on What Matters Most

In recent years, the concept of the servant leader has become more commonly used. It is not unusual for a well-known CEO, when asked about his leadership style, to hesitate for a second, look earnestly into the camera, and acknowledge they are all about serving. At the end of the interview, however, it is often unclear what they really mean by "serving."

Like most leadership approaches and philosophies, servant leadership is not a recent creation. The increasing interest around it, though, has produced a broader range of descriptors and practices with more and more leaders describing themselves with the label. Perhaps more so than any other leadership approach, servant leadership is defined more by a core belief than a specific set of outward expressions. Mark Miller, Vice President of High Performance Leadership at Chick-fil-A, and author Randy Gravitt, both thought leaders in this area, define it this way, "a leader compelled by an unshakeable desire to serve." Leaders who lack that core belief are not servant leaders but rather using some servant leadership practices among the many in their toolkits. The result may be not only an improvement in their leadership, but also increased frustration among their team. This occurs when team members feel that their deeds fall short of the promises and expectations associated with a true servant leader.

Notice we are not describing a servant but a servant leader. Servants generally don't have a choice, but a servant leader, through humility, chooses to put others first. Individuals often struggle with the practical application of servant leadership because it can sound like they will be overwhelmed trying to satisfy every need of those they lead. But leaders who do this well focus on where they can bring the most value to others. Leaders have limited time, resources, and energy, as well as limited areas of expertise and experience. When you serve your team, you initially spend time learning the aspirations, abilities, and needs of each member. From that understanding, a servant leader can make the highest value investment in each person.

Servant leadership also helps us to distinguish between a leader's skills and character. It can be easy to only see the leader's skills; the way they communicate, make decisions, and influence others, but to really see their character and heart takes time. Our initial impression of a leader, based on them possessing a high level of skills, often leads us to follow them because it looks like a likely path to success. However, when we discover the leader is self-serving by taking all the credit and rewards while failing to invest in others, we quickly see those same leadership skills as a detriment to the team. But when we see someone step up in a difficult situation despite the probability of failure and commit themselves wholly because it is the right thing to do, we are more likely to join with them for the long journey.

The unconditional nature of serving may be the most defining quality of this leadership approach. The leader's steadfastness to serve others cannot be dependent on the benefit they will receive or the individual's ability to produce the desired result. Servant leaders understand the imperfections of the ones they serve and of themselves. However, servant leadership is not synonymous with soft leadership. The deep desire to see each person reach their full potential requires the leader to carry that burden and be fully present in every encounter. It is the enduring quality of unconditional love that makes the bond between the servant leader and those they lead so powerful.

Practicing this leadership approach enables a leader to equally value results and relationships, which is one of the hardest things for leaders to do well. It starts with shifting from the more common question "How can I be successful?" to the much more significant question "How can I be of value to the people I lead?"

In a story, it's usually easier for us to see the full picture. In Reeves' case, at least on the surface, he did not seem very skillful at leadership. He was prone to misunderstandings and not apparently academically minded. His character, though, was always focused on serving others. He wanted nothing more than to help Schuster with whatever problem Dean Northum had laid on him that week. With each experience, Reeves expanded his ability to positively influence others as a servant leader.

Schuster is also a work in progress to become the servant leader he wants to be. Like many of us, when provided with the opportunity to serve, he can usually be expected to respond reluctantly. Yet, we see in him a deep commitment to the school, his students, and certainly to Reeves. Each story concluded with growth for both the teacher and the student; the leader and the follower.

In these five stories, we have explored skill areas that are critical for leading effectively and provided some foundational principles and best practices that allow all of us to grow in our leadership. Hopefully, you have also seen that the most effective application of these skills will be enhanced through a desire to serve others.

Further Reading

Servant Leadership: A Journey into the Nature of Legitimate Power and Greatness, Robert Greenleaf

The Secret: What Great Leaders Know and Do, Ken Blanchard and Mark Miller

Authors' Note

We hope you enjoyed discovering some of the principles and tools from our NextGen Global Leadership Series through the adventures of Reeves and Schuster. If you would like to learn how you can go deeper on these topics through our leadership blogs, workshops, and online academy, please visit www. rsleadershiplessons.com.

NextGen Leadership Topics

- Thriving in Change
- Communicating with Impact
- Creating Desirable Outcomes
- Delivering Innovative Solutions
- Discovering Opportunities in Every Decision
- Leveraging Strategic Insights
- Leading a Coaching Conversation
- The Leadership Conversation

We would also love to hear directly from you about what you are learning in your leadership journey.

Please contact us at:

sam.collins@lead-international.com

steve.collins@lead-international.com

About the Authors

Stephen Collins has spent over 30 years focusing on leadership and business development in a variety of global locations, and currently serves as Director of Global Training for LEAD International. After living overseas for 25 years, he now resides in Richmond, Virginia but still travels to equip leaders wherever they are striving to make a positive impact on their communities and organizations.

Sam Collins is an author/screenwriter who currently works as a producer, content-creator, and editor for LEAD International. He was born in Hong Kong, grew up in Jordan, and now enjoys spending time in the mountains of Virginia.

Business Books

Business Books publishes practical guides
and insightful non-fiction for beginners and professionals.
Covering aspects from management skills, leadership and
organizational change to positive work environments, career
coaching and self-care for managers, our books are a valuable
addition to those working in the world of business.

Recent Bestsellers from Business Books are:

From 50 to 500
Jonathan Dapra, Richard Dapra and Jonas Akerman
An engaging and innovative small business leadership
framework guaranteed to strengthen a
leader's effectiveness to drive company growth and results.
Paperback: 978-1-78904-743-1 ebook: 978-1-78904-744-8

Be Visionary
Marty Strong
Be Visionary: Strategic Leadership in the Age of Optimization
demonstrates to existing and aspiring
leaders the positive impact of applying visionary creativity
and decisiveness to achieve spectacular
long-range results while balancing the day-to-day.
Paperback: 978-1-78535-432-8 ebook: 978-1-78535-433-5

Finding Sustainability
Trent A. Romer
Journey to eight states, three national parks and three
countries to experience the life-changing
education that led Trent A. Romer to find sustainability for his
plastic-bag manufacturing business and himself.
Paperback: 978-1-78904-601-4 ebook: 978-1-78904-602-1

Inner Brilliance, Outer Shine
Estelle Read
Optimise your success, performance, productivity and
well-being to lead your best business life.
Paperback: 978-1-78904-803-2 ebook: 978-1-78904-804-9

Tomorrow's Jobs Today
Rafael Moscatel and Abby Jane Moscatel
Discover leadership secrets and technology strategies being
pioneered by today's most innovative
business executives and renowned brands across the globe.
Paperback: 978-1-78904-561-1 ebook: 978-1-78904-562-8

Secrets to Successful Property Investment
Deb Durbin
Your complete guide to building a property portfolio.
Paperback: 978-1-78904-818-6 ebook: 978-1-78904-819-3

The Effective Presenter
Ryan Warriner
The playbook to professional presentation success!
Paperback: 978-1-78904-795-0 ebook: 978-1-78904-796-7

The Beginner's Guide to Managing
Mikil Taylor
A how-to guide for first-time managers adjusting to their new
leadership roles.
Paperback: 978-1-78904-583-3 ebook: 978-1-78904-584-0

Forward
Elizabeth Moran
A practical playbook for leaders to guide their teams through
their organization's next big change.
Paperback: 978-1-78279-289-5 ebook: 978-1-78279-291-8

Readers of ebooks can buy or view any of these bestsellers by clicking on the live link in the title. Most titles are published in paperback and as an ebook. Paperbacks are available in traditional bookshops. Both print and ebook formats are available online.
Find more titles and sign up to our readers' newsletter at http://www.jhpbusiness-books.com/
Follow us on Facebook Read to Succeed with John Hunt Publishing